MAKING GRATEFUL KIDS

Making
Grateful
Kids

The Science of Building Character

JEFFREY J. FROH and GIACOMO BONO

TEMPLETON PRESS

Templeton Press
300 Conshohocken State Road, Suite 500
West Conshohocken, PA 19428
www.templetonpress.org

In some cases names have been changed to protect the identity
of the people addressed in the book.

Designed and typeset by Gopa & Ted2, Inc.

Library of Congress Cataloging-in-Publication Data on file.

Printed in the United States of America

14 15 16 17 18   10 9 8 7 6 5 4 3 2 1

To my wife, Cara, and children, James and Julianne,
my three greatest sources of gratitude.
—Jeffrey Froh

To the greatest joys of my life: my wife, Kate,
and my sons, Dario and Alex.
—Giacomo Bono

Contents

MAKING GRATEFUL KIDS

What Drives a Child Who Thrives?

*M*ATTHEW, a twelve-year-old middle school student who lives within a wealthy suburb, had a home life quite different than that of his peers: he and his mother had found themselves in a long-term shelter because of a financial crisis, and Matthew had to commute to school by public bus rather than the expensive cars his friends' parents used to drop their children off. As winter approached, Matthew continued to come to school dressed in jeans and T-shirts with just a thin sweatshirt for covering, prompting one teacher, Mrs. Riebe, to give him a wool sports jacket from the donation bin at her church. It was a kind gesture, but a sixth grader wearing a sport jacket in a prosperous public school means one thing: a bully target. Matthew, however, wasn't bullied, nor was he embarrassed about wearing an oversized jacket. Instead, he smiled from ear to ear. "Check out this cool jacket Mrs. Riebe gave me, I love it. I can't stop thanking her," he'd say to his friends and other teachers. His infectious positivity was so appealing even other kids recognized and respected it.

The circumstances in which Matthew lived might make many children feel envious, cheated, angry, and resentful. Yet Matthew felt incredibly grateful to his teachers and friends because his mother, despite the constraints on her time and finances, had instilled a sense of gratitude in Matthew; and this had a profound effect on his approach to life. We've collected nearly two thousand essays on what gratitude means to teens, Matthew's essay among them. He wrote, "My life wouldn't be the same without the people who've helped me succeed. I'm thankful to God and my family, friends, and even my teachers for helping me improve my life."

This story of an adolescent who lives below the material standards of most of his peers and has to make much more of an effort to get to school and participate in extracurricular activities is a small but profound example of the power that gratitude can have on a young person's emotional well-being, relationships, spirituality, and success. In fact, our experience as counselors and researchers working with at-risk children and adolescents supports this assumption. But Matthew is no ordinary kid because he has learned to harness a virtue that's been long-revered, but historically underappreciated: gratitude.

What Is Gratitude?

Gratitude is the appreciation people feel when somebody has done something kind or helpful for them or when they recognize the good things and people they have in their lives. Robert Emmons defines it as "a sense of thankfulness and joy in response to receiving a gift, whether the gift be a tangible benefit from a specific other or a moment of peaceful bliss evoked by natural beauty." Gratitude can be considered an emotion, a mood, or a personality trait. As a personality trait, gratitude is considered a life orientation to notice and appreciate the positive in life. Gratitude helps forge individuals' character by aligning their actions with their moral feelings and beliefs in the short run and their social relationships with their goals and ultimate concerns in the long run.

When people are grateful they commonly express thanks verbally or physically (a hug or handshake, even tears) toward those responsible. Gratitude alerts people to the valuable relationships in their lives, it reinforces the kindness of their benefactors, and it motivates them to reciprocate kindness to their benefactors or even extend kindness to others. Its experience and practice promotes positive social relationships with others and nurtures trusting relationships, benefiting society at large.

Despite the major role gratitude plays in people's well-being and success, there's been little research addressing its development and enhancement in children's lives. Psychoanalytic theories—which assume that individuals must repress unconscious impulses, anxieties, and internal conflicts to free up psychic energy and mature— were the first to try to explain gratitude development in children. Melanie Klein, the late Austrian-born British psychologist, wrote in her landmark 1957 book, *Envy and Gratitude: A Study of Unconscious Sources*, that gratitude first emerged in the earliest stages of infancy, but only if envy didn't overpower its development. Although later research hasn't supported Klein's findings, linguistic research from the 1970s and 80s found that kids' spontaneous expressions of thanks increased as they mature and age.

Despite its shortcomings, the limited but pioneering research into gratitude has blazed a trail for contemporary gratitude researchers like us. After reviewing the psychological literature on gratitude in young people, we found noticeable holes that needed to be filled. One such hole was the lack of research on gratitude in the early stages of life. Until 2005, there were no studies that we knew of examining gratitude and well-being in children. Then, in 2006, psychology professors and researchers Nansook Park and Christopher Peterson conducted a content analysis of parents' descriptions of children's strengths, gratitude being one. They found that out of the twenty-four strengths examined, gratitude had the strongest relationship to life satisfaction.

Excited by this finding, Jeff contacted the world's leading authority on gratitude, Robert Emmons, a University of California, Davis, psychology professor, to see if he would be interested in replicating an experiment that he and colleague Michael McCullough, director of the Evolution and Human Behavior Laboratory at the University of Miami, had conducted in 2003 about the beneficial effects of gratitude on adults who kept a gratitude journal. Except this time, the research participants would be adolescents. While it's true that some people are inherently more or less grateful than others, we were convinced that, regardless of where you fall on the gratitude meter, gratitude could be improved because it's expandable. Emmons agreed, and the replication went on to provide initial evidence that keeping a gratitude journal and counting blessings helped kids too. Soon thereafter, Emmons introduced Jeff to Giacomo (who had also been collaborating with Emmons). It was at this point that the two of us discovered our shared passion for understanding the science behind making kids more grateful, an endeavor we consider worthy given the prospect that the practice of gratitude could have lasting social benefits for a person long into adulthood.

In our initial conversations, that's exactly what we thought about. Could gratitude developed at a young age lead to greater overall happiness, supportive relationships, a sense of belonging and community, and hope for the future? Surprisingly, there was no evidence or study for this. We wondered if gratitude had particular benefits for kids' development—such as the belief that you have something important to offer others, a less materialistic attitude, or a sense of meaning and purpose. Again, we found no evidence that anyone had studied this in children. We were surprised that, outside of the counting blessings study with students mentioned above, there was no research on the best way for kids to develop and practice gratitude—and the potential outcomes of this effort. Clearly, this was an area of focus that needed attention, particularly because a great deal of evidence pointed to a variety of benefits of being a grateful adult, including improved behaviors for physical health, better mental health, and psychological as well as social well-being.

Two recent longitudinal studies indicate why gratitude may be particularly beneficial to youngsters. One study linked gratitude to greater social support, both perceived and actual, and protection from stress and depression over time. A second study, of an actual gift-giving event among sororities, showed that beneficiaries (new sisters) were most grateful when they felt understood, valued, and cared for by a benefactor (veteran sisters) and that this predicted later increases in both parties' sense of connection to each other as well as beneficiaries' sense of connection to the sorority overall. These results suggest that gratitude not only helps people form, maintain, and strengthen supportive relationships, but it also helps them feel connected to a caring community that values their contributions. Such assets are critical to the resilience and healthy development of children and adolescents.

Aside from several isolated studies that preceded current theorizing on gratitude, the study of gratitude in youth is in its infancy. Generally speaking, however, the emerging evidence from our research supports many of the advantages mentioned above among younger populations. To pique your interest, we've found that grateful young adolescents (ages 11–13), compared to their less grateful counterparts, are happier; are more optimistic; have better social support from friends and family; are more satisfied with their school, family, community, friends, and themselves; and give more emotional support to others. They're also physically healthier and report fewer physical symptoms such as headaches, stomachaches, and runny noses. We've also found that grateful teens (ages 14–19), compared to less grateful teens, are more satisfied with their lives, use their strengths to better their community, are more engaged in their schoolwork and hobbies, have higher grades, and are less envious, depressed, and materialistic.

Yet, the scientific view of gratitude as a human strength will remain incomplete without understanding how gratitude develops and helps an individual early on in development. After conducting several more gratitude studies with young people, we realized that gratitude is a quality that could be learned and strengthened with practice. *Making Grateful Kids* shares groundbreaking findings from our research and provides a comprehensive view of how to help kids find greater satisfaction, fulfillment, and meaning via gratitude.

This book explains how to create an environment that encourages children to develop thankfulness, and offers concrete, scientifically based strategies for making children and adolescents more appreciative, including building nurturing relationships, limiting screen time and exposure to media, connecting to a larger purpose, and so on. In fact, you can test the effectiveness of these strategies by measuring the gratitude of your child or adolescent before and after you apply the strategies. Because children learn many behaviors by observing and imitating adults, we also suggest that *you* apply the strategies in this book to yourself, too. You can measure your own gratitude before and after you use the strategies to see how effective they are in increasing your gratitude. The material in the appendix helps you measure gratitude formally via several scientifically validated gratitude questionnaires.

But you can also measure gratitude in your child and yourself informally. You can do this by noting specific thoughts and behaviors common to grateful people. For instance, instead of forgetting to notice your partner warming up your car before work, gratitude now fills your heart with love because your partner did this despite also having to rush out to work. Maybe your child says "thank you" more often now. Maybe your list of daily blessings quadrupled because you now feel grateful for small things like the sun keeping you warm as you wait for your child to get off of the bus. And maybe your child now hugs and thanks you for things he previously took for granted, such as you preparing his favorite dinner or leaving a special snack in his lunch bag.

Parents, teachers, pastors, counselors, and anyone who works with young people can use these ideas and strategies, grounded in the latest scientific research, to boost gratitude in children and adolescents. In *Making Grateful Kids*, we distill our cutting-edge and most compelling research findings on gratitude, some of which are still unpublished, and share real-life stories from adults and young people alike. By helping kids tune into and appreciate the daily gifts in their lives (e.g., friends who offered emotional support, teachers who gave up their lunch period to provide extra help, parents who stayed up late to help with a science project), we hope to strengthen their feelings of closeness and commitment to each other, to their teachers, families, and communities, and even to society.

What Good Is Gratitude?

Seventeen-year-old Scott exemplifies some findings from our four-year longitudinal studies on gratitude development in teens, which is described in detail throughout this book. Scott is well-known among both peers and adults for his conduct. For example, he sometimes skips school and, when he does go to school, getting sent to the principal's office for discipline is business as usual. He can also be a bit of a bully in an effort to get others to do what he wants.

Would you mind if Scott lived in your community? What if he attended the same school as your child? Would this bother you?

Maybe not so much—after all, he's just one apple in the bunch. But what if Scott lived on your street? Would you be okay with Scott and your child being friendly? Probably not. How about if he were a close friend of your child? Most definitely not—and we're with you on this.

But is Scott a lost cause? Should society throw up its hands in despair and give up? Our research suggests no. Indeed, we've found that kids like Scott can start changing their ways with increased gratitude. Moreover, grateful kids are proactively social and other-centered; they're always looking to join in, lend a hand to others, and spread kindness. They also possess many other special qualities—sticking up for others when they're teased, enjoying and actively participating in school, and being trustworthy—that make people want to have them in their lives. So one way to transform kids' character, and the science backs us up on this, is to make them more grateful.

What to Expect from Developing a Grateful Personality

There are four qualities that distinguish highly grateful people from less grateful people: they experience gratitude (1) more *intensely* for a positive event, (2) more *frequently* throughout the day (3) with greater *density* for any given benefit (i.e., they are grateful to more people for every positive event), and (4) they have a wider *span* of benefits at any given time in their lives for which they're grateful (e.g., for being included in an activity or being defended by someone, for succeeding on a test or performing well in a game). Therefore, one way you'll know that your child and you are becoming more grateful after following the strategies in this book is that you'll both start to noticeably embody these four qualities.

Here's how your child may behave after you read and apply the strategies from *Making Grateful Kids*. Rather than your kind gesture of driving your daughter's friend to softball practice so they can play together going unnoticed, your daughter later thanks you and even sets the table for dinner without being asked. Instead of hearing "thanks" from your child as often as you hear, "Hey Mom, can I take out the garbage tonight?" you now hear it more regularly, sometimes even daily. Though your teenager usually forgets everyone who has helped him succeed, you're now surprised to hear him mention a long list of people he's grateful to for helping him get his first job. And while you thought that your child was only grateful for video games, candy, or extra time watching cartoons, you notice her thanking you for a fun day at the beach or for encouraging her to keep trying when things got challenging. As you can see, every day could be quite different with gratitude in the picture. Having such experiences would truly be rewarding, and watching your child's behaviors transform into those that characterize a grateful person will be nothing short of magical.

Committing to First Things First

> "Most of us spend too much time on what is urgent and not enough time on what is important." —Stephen Covey, author of The 7 Habits of Highly Effective People

The approach to raising children we prescribe works, but it requires dedication. Managing life's demands makes it easier to prioritize making grateful kids. As the late educator and author Stephen Covey reminded us, "The main thing is for the main thing to remain the main thing." Successfully making grateful children requires you to: (1) believe making a grateful kid is a worthy goal, (2) learn what you need to do, (3) put weekly or even daily effort into it, and (4) commit to this goal for a long period of time—as in a regular part of raising your child.

Imagine that you have in front of you a big empty container, a pile of rocks of different sizes, a bag of sand, and a bucket of water. If you placed medium-sized rocks in the container, could you fit more stuff into it? Sure. You could fit small rocks. Now, once you add small rocks to the container, do you think there's space for more stuff? Yes. You can pour sand in there. Now that the sand has fallen between all of the rocks and filled up the remaining spaces, do you think you can add even more stuff to the container? Absolutely. You can add water.

We'll now present you with several big rocks. The million-dollar question is this: How do you get the big rocks into the container now that it's packed to the brim with stuff? Put the book down and really process this. We'll wait.

Okay, let's see if you got it right. The correct answer is: *you put the big rocks in first!* This is the metaphor Covey uses to drive home the importance of prioritizing. The big rocks represent your priorities in life, those things that matter most to you (e.g., relationships, health, and spiritual growth). All the other stuff represents life (e.g.,

responsibilities, chores, crises). If we don't identify those big rocks, such as making a grateful child, and fit them into our lives, nobody else will—and the windows for such choices will eventually close.

The illustration reminds us that the things that matter most must never take a back seat to things that matter least. That is, our goal of making a grateful child should be more important than meeting other people's priorities or expectations and needless interruptions like social media and television.

· · · · ·

The effort to make your children grateful is worth it. You'll have a better family life, and you'll provide a great foundation for your children to enter the world, ready to flourish into caring adults. Moreover, by helping even our youngest citizens become more naturally appreciative, we'll make kids more receptive to everything the world has to offer, including what they can learn from their teachers, parents, friends, community, and nature—creating an upward spiral of positivity resulting in even more gratitude.

CHAPTER 1

Orienting Your Family toward Gratitude

*G*RATITUDE should spring from the first supportive relationships in a child's life, such as with parents and caregivers and, eventually, from other close relationships. Indeed, our research shows that youth with supportive and satisfying family and peer relationships are more grateful. Yet even in homes that actively encourage gratitude, a young person's ability to reason and accept challenging situations varies with maturity. One day, Giacomo's seven-year-old son Dario noticed his little brother Alex had been given a new toy. It quickly dawned on Dario that he didn't have the same good fortune, and he swiftly made his displeasure known to his mother. He then cried, but not without saying that it just wasn't fair—a sentiment he repeated many times. Many of you may chuckle at this scenario because you've experienced it with your kids. And there's good reason. Children argue about who has more, or better, toys. But why? Why is it so easy for kids—and adults—to focus on things to complain about?

Encourage Your Kids to Tune into Positive Emotions

Emotions give us important information about our environment. If we feel anxious, it may be because we sense a looming threat. If we feel angry, it may be because someone frustrated us or hurt us. But when we're happy, we don't always think about why. When it comes to positive emotions, we usually just enjoy the feeling because positive emotions signal to us that the current circumstances are going well, so we should just continue doing what we're doing to reap more of the same. As a result, we automatically tend to be less analytical during positive states and fail to focus on the reasons why they came to happen. During negative events, on the other hand, we tend to analyze things more. Our nature compels us to figure out why negative events transpire so that we might, in the future, avoid or prevent them entirely. While this state of affairs generally helps us survive, it doesn't necessarily help us thrive. So let's revisit Dario and Alex with this in mind.

Let's say Dario came home to discover new toys for both he and his brother. It would be easy to imagine him ripping open his gift in record time then delving eagerly into playing with it without considering why he even got the toy. This natural tendency becomes especially ingrained in adults. Like Dario, we tend to not think about why good things come our way. But if his mom first asked Dario to explain why Alex and he received toys that day, he would likely make the connection between the reward—the toys—and the boys' good behavior—cleaning up after playtime all week.

The more we understand why positive events happen for us, the easier it is to tune into possible sources of gratitude (at least when people are responsible for those events). In this example, mom helps her kids feel good for being responsible, they appreciate getting toys from her, and everybody is content with this good state of affairs. This leads us to the first strategy: capitalize on positive emotions. It can be useful with kids as young as three years old.

 STRATEGY 1: Focus children on *why* good things happen to them and on the people responsible for making the good things happen.

This basic strategy helps initiate discussions with children that can help them notice and understand how others were purposefully involved in helping them. To employ this strategy, an adult and child should talk about the good things that happened during the day (or a week) and, why, in the child's opinion, those good things happened. This guides the child to notice a friend or teacher for his kindness. For example, a child might say that she learned a fun new game in school from a friend who showed her how to play. The parent can take this opportunity to suggest the child appreciate her friend for including her in the fun.

Gratitude aids humans' survival because it helps people identify the relationships that are personally more important to them than others. This strategy is useful in many settings. For instance, being thankful and appreciative of people who have been helpful and kind can easily be encouraged in school. This practice could also complement other exercises to help stoke a more cooperative classroom environment.

At home, children could think about the blessings of the day or week to come up with more thoughtful prayers. This could be done at mealtime, and our longitudinal data show that children who say grace during meals have also developed more gratitude than their peers. You could encourage children to give thanks to all the people responsible for the food on the table, which could include farmers, fishermen, truck drivers, supermarket employees, and God. You could also encourage your children during prayer at bedtime to be thankful for the people who have recently helped them or been good to them and to thank God for having such special people in their lives.

To test this strategy, Jeff and his colleagues Robert Emmons and William Sefick asked sixth and seventh graders to keep a daily journal for two weeks. The students were divided into three groups. The first group was instructed to write about five things they were grateful for; the second group was asked to focus on hassles. The third group functioned as a control, and the students in it simply completed the questionnaire administered to all three groups.

Students writing in gratitude journals made entries such as:

* "My coach helped me out at baseball practice."
* "My grandma is in good health, my family is still together, my family still loves each other, my brothers are healthy, and we have fun every day."
* "I am grateful that my mom didn't go crazy when I accidentally broke a patio table."

Students writing about hassles made entries such as:

* "I hate when people act like idiots and make fun of others."
* "I had to get up early for soccer, and we lost the game because I missed a penalty shot."
* "I feel like I'm trying so hard in school to do well but it's not enough."

Our research found that students who counted their blessings became more grateful, optimistic, satisfied with their lives and experienced fewer negative emotions. Three weeks after keeping their gratitude journals, students who counted blessings said that they were grateful for school and their education and reported feelings of greater satisfaction with their school. They also reported they were learning more and were eager to go to school.

The benefits of this change in perspective are very real. Students who are satisfied with school get better grades and have stronger social relationships; and encouraging students to count their blessings may help them think more positively about school in general and academics more specifically. Teachers know this. We've heard numerous testimonies of teachers putting this strategy into practice. For instance, teachers sometimes install gratitude boards or walls in their classrooms. Students add notes or pictures of things or people they appreciate, of their achievements, or of significant places or experiences. Smart coaches also apply the strategy by using cooperative skill building drills and then encouraging kids to thank any team mates for helping them improve their skills.

Learning to Appraise Beneficial Social Exchanges

Let's dig deeper to understand why this first strategy is an effective starting point for making grateful kids. When we direct our gratitude to others, we become more tuned into the relationships in our lives that are supportive, fulfilling, and mutually reinforcing—the kind of relationships that create a special environment for beneficial circumstances to occur. This knowledge helps us improve our ability to gain assistance or cooperation from others. Promoting gratitude as a basic social skill for your kids teaches them in turn to pay the same kind of attention to positive elements and people in their lives, creating good feelings and enhancing their learning experiences. The earlier and more often in life we employ this strategy with children, the more open they'll be to becoming grateful, and, as we'll learn in later chapters, the better their chances of achieving success, well-being, and coherence about their particular life story and all the people involved.

Help Kids Deal with Negative Emotions

Between the preschool years and middle childhood (ages 3–12), children tend to think in black-and-white terms, and they have unrealistic perspectives based mostly on their own needs at any given time. For example, when Jeff and his wife set limits on how long their son, James, can play his Wii game system by saying, "We'll let you play for more time than usual today, but then you can't play tomorrow," James fires back with, "You always take away the Wii from me," throwing his hands up in despair. In James's mind, a Saturday without playing Wii clearly indicates his parents are ruthless dictators with no concern for his interests (ignoring the fact that they allowed more playtime Friday night and promised a little more on Sunday). You may be wondering what can be done to manage such perceptions of unfairness, given how frequently they occur in most households. This leads us to the second strategy, which is the other side of the emotional coin as compared to the first strategy: how to help kids deal with negative emotions.

 STRATEGY 2: Help children regulate negative emotions by being a calm problem solver, by labeling and validating their emotions, and by replacing their negative thoughts with positive ones.

As you might expect, this second strategy is much more difficult than the first one to employ. Life can be filled with disappointments. This is true for adults, but it's especially true for children. Growing up is hard work. Every day is packed with novelty and challenges as they move forward faster than their limited knowledge base and cognitive skills can handle. Helping children learn to manage their emotions is critical and may be one of the greatest challenges of parenting. So for instance, even though Jeff and his wife are both school psychologists and try their hardest not to foster perfectionism, their six-year-old son James is very hard on himself when he makes mistakes. When Jeff beats him in chess, James gets extremely upset, sometimes to the point of crying and saying things like "What was I thinking? I didn't even have a game plan!" Jeff will try to lighten things up with a hug and a reminder that no one is perfect and that making mistakes is part of life. Sometimes this calms James down, but sometimes it doesn't. The truth is there are no quick, one-size-fits-all solutions to handling negative emotions. Plenty of patience, creativity, and effort are required; and you can count on second-guessing, self-doubt, and occasional instances of guilt and shame happening to you along the way.

Modeling Good Problem Solving

Remaining calm is the first part of this strategy, as adults model healthy emotion regulation for children with their own behavior. Taking a deep breath and figuring out how to get by or finding a sufficient solution to the problem in the moment is an essential tool. When you feel pressured to get your child to soccer practice or a music lesson, it can be quite frustrating when he has a meltdown because he didn't get a chance to add another Lego to his supersonic airplane-submarine or color in one more giraffe on his animal safari masterpiece. A calm response from you shows him that you can help him through and that the problem isn't too hard to solve. Conversely, angrily tearing a child away from a project at the last minute demonstrates a loss of control on your part, and it also tells him that you didn't care about his project.

Though often unintentional, such adult behavior can cause harm nonetheless. And everybody is guilty of it. Take Giacomo, who did just this when his son Dario needed to get ready for baseball practice. After reminding his son to put on his shoes, each reminder louder than the last, Giacomo finds Dario, to his disbelief, playing blissfully on his Nintendo DS. When Giacomo tells him to, "Shut that thing off right now," Dario replies, "But wait, look, I'm about to beat the invisible Mario in the cart race, and I've never done that before!" Snatching the DS from him, Giacomo thunders, "I don't care about Mario—you were supposed to get your shoes on for practice!" If, instead of shouting reminders, Giacomo had anticipated better and checked on Dario sooner, he would have realized that none of the reminders actually registered and things could have been smoother that afternoon.

Even so, sometimes the chaos of life gets in the way. For instance, Jeff was once alone with both his kids, and he was running late to get his son on the bus. Of course it was at that moment that his three-year-old daughter, Julianne, insisted on buttoning her jacket herself. Anxious and frazzled that they were going to miss the bus, Jeff hastily buttoned Julianne's jacket while she cried, "I wanted to do it!" He picked her up as they left the house, and she proceeded to deliver several sharp kicks to his ribs while she threw a tantrum in his arms. Had he been able to remain calm, he might have instead told her that she could button her jacket when they got outside. But the morning rush got the best of him that time.

Even with our best intentions, we don't always keep our cool, and that's *okay*. Although consistently failing to be a calm problem solver can be counterproductive and harmful to kids in the long run, we believe that if you maintain a calm demeanor most of the time you will help instill gratitude in your kids. We have yet to confirm with research how this tool might be related to making children grateful, but we suspect it's helpful because it shows that you care about them and the things that they care about. Calm problem solving teaches persistence and demonstrates that working together leads to the best solutions. Believing that other people care about your welfare is an important source of gratitude. This will serve your children well when they establish friendships, social ties, or working relationships in the future. As calm problem solvers, your kids will be more in tune with others' needs and how to help them through their problems, strengthening the bonds that lead to continued success in the world.

We Understand Your Pain: Helping Kids Understand Negative Emotions

Labeling and validating children's emotions are crucial. When children are distressed or experiencing negative emotions, they may not understand why things didn't work out the way they wanted. They may be too frustrated by something happening unexpectedly, or they may be completely consumed by the fact or perception that they've been treated unfairly. During such moments it's important for parents to get to the bottom of why their child is sad, frustrated, or angry and help her understand what she's going through by helping her label negative emotions. In other words, you enrich your child's emotional vocabulary so that she can better communicate her feelings next time.

Negative emotions can be overwhelming for children because emotional competence is complex and only develops gradually as kids experience and adapt to different social contexts. Thus, it's also critical that adults validate, or show that they understand, the turmoil their kids are going through. This teaches children that disappointment is a normal part of life and that it's okay to feel the way they do. It also lets them know that they're not alone in their suffering. By giving children the verbal skills to express their negative emotions *and* by being affirming and supportive of them through their turmoil, adults help children develop healthy emotion regulation. These two skills transform negative emotional events into valuable learning experiences.

For example, a child may be drawing or coloring something and all of a sudden throw a tantrum that it's "completely ruined" because she went outside the lines or used the wrong color. This is a good occasion for adults to show they understand why she's frustrated and help her accomplish her goal. It's easy for an adult to step in and want to quickly deal with the matter by saying, "Don't worry about it, sweetie, it's just a picture. We have more paper you can use to do another." But in this instance, you might instead say something like, "I know you worked hard on this picture, I'd be upset too. Let's see what we can do to fix it." This latter approach validates the child's frustration, labels the emotional experience, and shows her that you support her in correcting the problem. It just takes a little empathy.

Labeling and validating children's emotions both support children's understanding of gratitude at a very young age. Helping children understand and talk about their own and other people's emotions and mental states play important roles in promoting gratitude early on in life, as recent research documents. Knowledge of emotions as young as age three leads to a greater understanding of thoughts and beliefs at age four, and these two factors are both linked to a better understanding of the concept of gratitude by age five.

Helping to Reframe Children's Negative Thoughts

Replacing children's negative thoughts with positive ones is the last tool in the second strategy. Psychologists call this tool "cognitive restructuring" or "positive reframing," and it can be used to produce gratitude in kids. Frustration and anger are incompatible with readiness for gratitude because negative emotions tend to constrict our focus to the causes of those experiences, and this prevents positive exchanges with others. So learning to cope with negative emotions is a necessary tool for kids to develop early on. As we discussed previously in the chapter, children must learn that their negative feelings are valid and be offered alternative positive solutions in a way that's acceptable to them. A key to positive reframing is figuring out how to get your child to understand and accept the alternatives as her own. So you'll need to draw on your creativity.

Sometimes this is easy. Let's go back to an earlier example. When Dario didn't get a new toy while his brother did, his mom simply reminded him of rewards he's earned in the past. She explained to him that he hadn't done his usual chores while his brother had and challenged him to do better next time by saying, "Dario, I understand you're upset that you didn't get a toy. But you didn't clean up this week to earn it, and I know you can do it because you cleaned up last week. So try better next week."

Notice that this response helps guide a child's attention by making clear that the adult supports him in trying to solve the problem and that he doesn't have to be a victim. Dario's focus moves from feeling he's been treated unfairly to feeling believed in and empowered—the more constructive view provided by his mom. But the truth is, Dario didn't accept the challenge this time, and instead he kept brewing in his perception that it was "just not fair." It's important, however, to try to replace negative thoughts regardless of the outcome. Sometimes it helps to wait and find a teachable moment later, once emotions have subsided, which is how this situation with Dario actually played out.

Dario's mom was walking him home from school the day after the toy incident when they encountered two brothers, friends of his at school. The boys mentioned that they wouldn't be attending the same school next year because their father had cancer and would be unable to work during his treatment. So they had to move because they wouldn't be able to afford the rent. Upon arriving home, Dario's mom took the opportunity to ask Dario if he thought the boys' situation was sad. He definitely agreed. She proceeded to point out that "we're so lucky to have a nice house and especially our health; these things are much more important than new toys." Dario agreed, and for the remainder of the discussion he seemed to really understand that "we should be grateful for the important things we have," even mentioning other things he was grateful for, like "Dad's cooking, because we can't survive without eating." Making comparisons with others who are less fortunate (known as "downward social comparisons") is a great way to positively reframe a child's complaint in a way that emphasizes gratitude.

Sometimes, though, it's possible to deal with a child's negative perspective more quickly and easily. One day the tables were reversed, and it was Dario's younger brother, Alex, who was upset because of "unfair" treatment. He came home from school one day and learned Dario was enjoying a special day with Grandma at Disneyland. Mom found a simple fix: she mentioned that Alex's turn to have a special day with Grandma would be the next day. This example shows that replacing a child's negative thoughts with an attractive alternative can calm his negative emotions. Unfortunately, one of the stresses and strains of parenting is that helping a child reframe unfair situations in a positive light is rarely so simple; nevertheless, it's well worth the effort because coping with negative emotions is especially difficult for children still learning the language and strategies to regulate their emotions.

Managing Emotions: Gratitude Grows During Positive Events

Let's take a moment to consider how the first two strategies we've mentioned work together to create good conditions for making kids grateful. Researchers have recently discovered that there's a 3:1

ratio, called the Losada Line, of positive-to-negative emotions kids need to flourish. Teaching kids to recognize their blessings helps increase the number of positive emotions they experience—and builds up the left side of their Losada Line. But things don't always turn out how we'd like, and kids are quick to notice. Even so, it's important to counter their negative appraisals as promptly as possible to help them cope effectively with negative events. Psychologists agree that we tend to spiral either upwards toward greater positivity and functioning or downwards toward greater negativity and dysfunction. Helping children reframe negative experiences into positive ones helps them avoid the dysfunctional pattern in later life.

We also habituate to events and experiences. That means an unusual circumstance may momentarily change our thoughts and feelings, but we soon return to our typical levels, or set-point, of positivity or negativity. For example, let's say that a teenager's happiness set-point is seven out of ten (with higher levels indicating greater happiness) and that he was just accepted by his top college choice. At first, he'll be exhilarated, with a happiness level of nine out of ten. He'll tell all his friends, call Grandma in Florida, and maybe even show the world by broadcasting it over social media. But over time, perhaps a few months, his happiness level will return to seven.

According to Sonja Lyubomirsky, a renowned happiness researcher and professor of psychology at the University of California, Riverside, there are two requirements for making sustainable gains in happiness: slowing down the rate of return to our set-point after positive events and speeding up our return to our set-point after negative events. Thus, the basic habits of emotional management we've been discussing help produce mindfulness for the positive elements in life—stretching out one's happiness on one hand—and they help produce healthy coping for the negative elements in life—reducing one's distress on the other hand. They also provide a general orientation for helping adults maintain an attitude of gratitude, which we turn to now.

 STRATEGY 3: To make a grateful kid, learn to manage your own emotional experiences first. Do this by moving quickly past the negative events and stretching out the positive events.

Get a Handle on Things Before It's Too Late

To effectively implement strategies 1 and 2 with kids—and all of the strategies in this book, actually—you must first put these two strategies into practice yourself. Maintaining a reserve of positivity and keeping your negative emotions in check will give you the mental and emotional resources necessary to apply what you learn from this book. Let's start with managing negative emotions. Believe it or not, a child knows if an adult dishes out a harsher punishment than her misbehavior actually deserves. If an adult screams at her to, "Stop yelling!" she may stop for the moment out of fear, but she'll learn more from your behavior than your words. She'll come to think that by yelling or talking over someone she can get her way, and that this is how stuff gets accomplished. As you can imagine, this is counterproductive in the long run, making it a sure way to lose the kind of deep connection we're encouraging in this book, which is what's needed if we are to make a kid grateful.

Basically, kids have a pretty good sense of when adults are not in control. So it's critical that adults learn to manage their negative emotions and be mindful of whether kids are present before venting. It's fine for kids to see you handle frustrations and conflicts constructively. So when you and your partner want to have a serious conversation about having another child, moving, or some other life-altering situation, don't feel like you need to shield your kids from the conversation. Have the talk. Be passionate about your stance even. But don't let kids see you lose it. You'll be setting an example you don't want them to emulate. Kids are always watching—and imitating—so use the pause button before you lose control.

When it comes to managing negative emotions, conflict resolution skills certainly would be good to have, as would stress-reduction techniques. It's important to figure out how to manage negative emotions, not just for the sake of the kids around you, but for the sake of your own health and well-being too. Sustained negative emotions—especially anger, resentment, and hostility—are detrimental to your health and can cause coronary heart disease. They're also toxic and spread to others, making it less likely that you'll be able to personally experience gratitude, much less model these behaviors or put into action many of the other strategies laid out in this book. Remember, learning to regulate negative emotions and manage negative events more effectively and quickly is important for living the good life, which will put you in the mental and emotional state needed to make your child grateful.

Expanding Positive Events and Thriving

The positivity–negativity ratio we discussed earlier applies in other areas of life, too. It affects well-being and performance for teams at work and in sports, families, and partners in wedlock. Put simply, how people work together starts to break down if there are an insufficient number of positive interactions or too many negative interactions.

John Gottman, emeritus professor at the University of Washington, found what he called a "magic ratio" of 5:1 for married couples experiencing positive and negative interactions. By observing seven hundred individual newlywed couples' interactions for fifteen minutes, he and his colleagues were able to predict with a 94 percent success rate which couples would stay together and which would get divorced based on how much couples engaged in criticism, contempt, defensiveness, and withdrawal while discussing important matters.

So it's a safe bet to monitor the quality of your interactions. One of the silent enemies of happiness in modern life is busyness. In the toil of life we simply forget to listen actively, provide help, or say thanks to others. It's therefore helpful to get into the habit of reminding yourself to do this. It'll be worth it, and you'll be glad you did as you watch your relationships strengthen and flourish.

You could also make a daily ritual of doing a simple kind act, such as making coffee for your partner in the morning, or expressing gratitude to friends, relatives, and coworkers. It's important to be genuine and realistic with what you can do. Start small. Setting the bar too high will lead to frustration or giving up altogether. You can always add on later. We also suggest you keep a journal about your experience with these new relationship-enhancing behaviors as a way of charting how your relationships have consequently improved. This will likely give way to writing and thinking about gratitude.

But aside from listing what you're grateful for and why, you could also write about how things would be without a positive person in your life. For example, you could write about how life might have been different if you never met your spouse. Maybe you wouldn't be a parent, maybe you would live in a different community, or maybe you would have a different job. Acknowledging the tremendous impact your partner has had on you will make you feel even more grateful for his or her presence in your life. To increase the chances that you stick with writing in your journal, you should designate a time of day that works best for you. Recording such things will help you stretch out your focus on the sources of happiness in your life, giving you the energy to implement the strategies in this book to make your child grateful.

 STRATEGY 4: Take care of yourself. You matter too.

Many parents struggle with balancing their own needs with their kids' needs. We think, incorrectly, that if we pour everything we've got into parenting—sacrificing time for our own exercise, sleep, stress management, hobbies, life planning, relationship building, value clarification, and spiritual development—our kids will flourish. Talk about being dead wrong! By neglecting ourselves and not engaging in self-care, not only are we on the road to languishing, but, ironically, we're also setting our kids up to languish too. The reason is simple. Our bodies are like ecosystems, consisting of four dimensions: physical, mental, social/emotional, and spiritual. Every dimension affects the others, so neglecting one dimension will negatively impact the rest. To have the energy and focus needed to raise grateful kids, we *must* get into the habit of tending to all aspects of our personal development.

Nurturing Ourselves

Tony Schwartz, CEO of the Energy Project and author of *Be Excellent at Anything*, has some helpful ideas about self-care. In fact, he's developed a business around personal energy management based on these ideas and is now helping companies like Google, Coca-Cola, the Los Angeles Police Department, Sony, and Genentech apply them to improve their bottom lines and the quality of life for their employees. His idea is refreshingly simple: we can't replenish the amount of time we have available to get things done, but we can replenish our energy. And he's not alone. A growing multidisciplinary body of research supports the idea that things like breaks, naps, more sleep, and more vacation actually help productivity. But how can you apply this to everyday life outside of work?

While your kids are playing outside and you're getting dinner ready, call a friend or crank up your favorite music; while you're waiting for your computer to boot up, meditate or read some scripture; or when your kids are finally asleep, spend time in active leisure, whether that's exercising, writing, or having adult time with your partner. Whatever you do, just be sure to replenish your energy. Obviously, this is tough for adults, especially parents with young children who have many needs. But what's important is that you find what restores you and make it fit your schedule and lifestyle. Remember, self-renewal isn't selfish. If anything, it's very other-centered because taking care of yourself will give you the vitality and determination needed to stay committed to the goal of making your child grateful.

Making a Habit out of Valuing Important Social Connections

A common theme you'll see throughout this book is the importance of helping children and teens create and maintain positive social relationships as a means to becoming more grateful. Similarly, if adults are to make grateful kids, they too must create and maintain healthy social relationships because they energize us and are the most reliable sources of gratitude. And if we're going to pass gratitude on to our kids, then we must also have it in our social lives.

When was the last time you were in a public space and didn't see several people with their faces glued to their smartphone or some other digital screen? Certainly, instant electronic access has many benefits in today's world. But science is starting to put up warning signs that a lifestyle lacking meaningful social connections to others is unhealthy and could even shorten a person's life.

Recent research by Barbara Fredrickson, Kenan Distinguished Professor of Psychology at the University of North Carolina, Chapel Hill, and her colleagues shows that maintaining meaningful social connections sharpens our ability to engage in such meaningful moments of personal contact, in the same way that physical exercise makes us stronger. In other words, "Your heart's capacity for friendship also obeys the biological law of 'use it or lose it.' If you don't regularly exercise your ability to connect face-to-face, you'll find yourself lacking some of the basic biological capacity to do so."

Research from Fredrickson and her colleagues also found that how much time people spend feeling attuned to others actually improves their vagal tone—the connection between the heart and the brain that enables smooth functioning of the internal organ system. Basically, the more positive social connections to others we have, the healthier we become.

For our purposes this suggests that parents and adults should pay more attention to the quality of social connection they have with children and with other adults—especially when children are around—because over time doing so optimizes the biology and psychology of everyone involved. Thus, in the electronic world we live in today, it's more important than ever to remember to unplug our children and ourselves and instead have some pleasant face-to-face social experiences together. We hope that this book helps you do this more deeply than ever.

CHAPTER 2

Raising Grateful Children from the Beginning

*G*ENUINE GRATITUDE involves an ability to appreciate a gift from a benefactor, whether that be a real person or something more spiritual—like God or the universe—as well as the motivation to return a favor or kind act. Although it's not until the ages of seven to ten that children begin to reliably understand gratitude in these terms, developmental research suggests that its primary precursors begin in infancy, the time when many other positive characteristics can also begin to grow. Our next strategies start there too—at the beginning of your son or daughter's new life.

 STRATEGY 5: Be a sensitive and responsive caregiver; be alert to children's needs, pay attention to their wants and interests, and provide prompt and warm responses that satisfy their needs.

Nurturing Secure Attachment

Love is the most important quality in the relationship between parent and child, and babies in their first year of life give parents ample opportunity to demonstrate their love. Fortunately, infants provide signals to parents for opportunities to show their love through two basic behavior systems—*novelty-seeking* and *proximity-seeking*. Both behavior systems aid infants' survival. When infants feel safe in their environment, they crawl around to explore their surroundings and play with new objects even though seeking novelty can be dangerous with a potential for injury. Thus, when the inevitable happens, and infants are frustrated, fearful, or hurt, their self-protecting proximity-seeking behavior kicks in and they quickly seek out an attachment figure for comfort or security.

Attachment is the deep and enduring emotional bond connecting one person to another. Consistently warm and positive interactions between parent and child promote secure attachment in children. That's why it's important for adults to respond to infants quickly by remaining accessible, learning the baby's cues, and being savvy about his or her favorite objects, activities, and games. Engaging in sensitive responsiveness—the essence of strategy 5—helps parents do this and keeps them tuned into the needs of the infant so that they can adjust their response if needed or continue the interactions initiated by the infant. By consistently addressing your child's needs this way, you help your baby establish a trusting and secure attachment to you, making it possible for your baby to form other secure attachments by the end of their first year.

Steering Clear of Insecure Attachment

Raising kids can be difficult even in the best of times, but it can be especially difficult when life gets stressful. Thus, it's helpful to consider the kinds of adult behaviors that in the long run create insecurely attached children who grow into insecure or unhappy adults.

Parents who are depressed or openly or subconsciously resentful of the demands of parenting are often emotionally unavailable to their children. Some parents hold the erroneous belief that responsiveness spoils a child. Such parents may even expect their child to be independent, and they rigidly control interactions in an effort to achieve this. Whatever the reason, parents who are regularly indifferent to their child's signals, ignore their needs, reject bids for attention, or respond harshly to their child's proximity-seeking tend to instill an insecure pattern of attachment in the child, known as *avoidant attachment*. Essentially, the child learns that he cannot expect to count on a parent and, therefore, doesn't bother even when distressed or in need.

Still, other parents may misjudge, fail to respond promptly, or be inconsistent in addressing their child's needs. A mother may not heed her daughter's cries of distress, for example, if she's preoccupied about issues at work. She might respond only after her daughter cries louder for attention. Over time, such a response, if consistent, teaches a child that her parent is not dependable when needed and that more intense proximity-seeking may change things. This pattern of parental behavior often leads to an insecure pattern of attachment referred to as *anxious-resistant*.

Knowing is half the battle, so if you recognize yourself in these descriptions, make the effort to reevaluate and change course to a sensitive and responsive style. This is the first step in making grateful kids.

One Secure Bond Brings a Lifetime of Benefits

Gratitude is strongly linked to interpersonal trust. When children develop a secure attachment with their parents, they're more likely to trust them and do the same with others. In turn, these attachments become *working models* for future relationships. Working models remain relatively stable from childhood to adulthood, so fostering a secure attachment with your child from the beginning helps him or her develop healthy emotions and social skills. For example, because you consistently followed through on your promises, your child learned to trust you. Now, as a teenager, he is willing to do what's necessary to keep his promises, see his commitments through, and enjoy loyal friendships, caring romantic relationships, and productive ties with teachers, mentors, and his community.

The groundbreaking Minnesota Longitudinal Study of Parents and Children, begun in 1975, found that preschoolers who were defined as *securely attached infants* were rated by teachers as more compliant to requests, competent at solving problems, and socially skilled than preschoolers who were defined as *insecurely attached infants*. At age ten, this pattern continued: these school-aged children were observed to have higher self-esteem and confidence, to be more self-reliant and resilient, and to have healthier friendships. Then, by adolescence, peers rated these children as more likeable, they showed more leadership qualities, and they reported more stable dating relationships. Infants who were securely attached even had more satisfying romantic relationships throughout adulthood.

It's not necessarily the case that all these outcomes are locked in place in the first years of life. They may also be due to parental sensitivity that continues as children grow. Nonetheless, these findings make a very strong case that one of the most important goals for parents is to help their child have a secure attachment with them and with other loved ones.

When the first relationships in a child's life are caring and filled with love, and when parents and caregivers continue to be sensitively responsive to that child, the child comes to view and approach other relationships—be it with teachers, peers, friends, or romantic partners—positively. Positive relationships are necessary for making grateful kids.

STRATEGY 6: Support children's autonomy by empathizing with them, using an authoritative parenting style, and letting them influence interactions.

Taking a Child's Point of View

The ability to take a child's point of view and consider how children experience events is an important part of positive parenting. Parents can better tune in empathetically to children by considering their physical needs (e.g., are they hungry, tired, or overstimulated?), emotional needs (e.g., can they adequately deal with their frustration or anger?), and personal desires (e.g., what are they trying to accomplish?). These considerations are what Ted Dix, associate professor at the School of Human Ecology, University of Texas, Austin, found help parents empathize with children. Parents with greater empathy toward children are more involved and nurturing with them. Regularly practicing empathy with children models empathy and increases their chances of learning when and how to use it.

A Parenting Style That Dances: Squeeze 'Em Tight and Show 'Em How

Besides tuning in, the *quality* of adults' interactions with children is also important. Developmental scholars sometimes characterize sensitive responsiveness as a dance in which the child is the lead partner because it involves paying attention to a child's cues of needs and wants, and then facilitating or helping them satisfy those needs and wants—but not to the point of taking over the interaction. There's no better way to understand how to do this than to heed the work of Diana Baumrind, a distinguished developmental psychologist at the University of California, Berkeley.

Baumrind found that parenting styles depend on different degrees of control and warmth. *Authoritarian parents* are high in control and low in warmth. They convey expectations for mature behavior and demand obedience from children. They provide guidelines for complying and consequences for not complying. And they expect children to respect their authority, do as they're told without discussion, and make mature decisions on their own. *Permissive/ indulgent parents* are low in control but high in warmth. They give children lots of love for their physical and emotional needs. But they provide few limits, few expectations for behaving maturely, and no consequences for not complying. These parents try too hard to be their kid's friend and tend to be neglectful when it comes to providing guidance and structure. *Authoritative parents* are high in control and high in warmth. They convey expectations for mature behavior and provide reasons and guidelines for complying. They provide consistent consequences for not complying. And they allow for discussion in the hope of steering children to making mature decisions on their own and accepting responsibility for the consequences of their behaviors.

Of these three parenting styles, authoritative parenting fares the best. It produces children who are high in competence and personal responsibility and who have healthy social relationships. The authoritarian style fares worse, producing children who are submissive and dependent, or hostile and rebellious. The permissive/indulgent style ranks in between these two, producing children who are less competent and assertive than peers raised with an authoritative style; these children also need approval from social relationships and disregard rules. There's also a fourth style, *neglectful parenting*. These parents reject or dismiss a child's needs and fail to provide rules or standards of behavior (low in control and low in warmth). This style fares even worse than authoritarian parenting, producing children rife with problems.

What our research suggests is that gratitude helps children develop into autonomous, socially competent, and purposeful individuals who are satisfied with their life. Because of its emphasis on the authentic needs and interests of children and its respect for children's autonomy, the authoritative style provides the kind of flexible provision of structure and support that promotes a child's capacity for gratitude. It also shows children that a parent or caregiver is clearly involved in their lives, invested in their welfare, and devoted to caring for them unconditionally, thus giving them more reasons to be grateful.

Let Your Child Lead the Way to Gratitude

A balance of child-directed and adult-directed interactions facilitates the process of instilling gratitude. Parents sometimes spend lots of energy trying to force children to play in a certain way or to play something they don't want to play. Though well intentioned, it's not being sensitive and responsive to the child. Allowing children to influence interactions, on the other hand, can be beneficial. For example, when Jeff's daughter, Julianne, was thirteen months old, she found it amusing to walk into her playhouse, shut the door, and wait for Jeff to ring the doorbell, to which she would respond "Heyyo" holding the toy phone to her ear. Though Jeff's head was spinning after several minutes of this and he was ready to move on to the swing set, he knew it was important to show Julianne that he was interested in the game she created because it demonstrated his appreciation and respect for her creativity and authenticity. With secure attachments, the relationship between child and adult starts to become more mutual, and both parties start trying to meet the other's respective goals and needs through the interactions. Thus, the last part of this sixth strategy helps boost parents' efforts to support their child's autonomy.

Together, the first strategies in this chapter provide guidelines for making the earliest and most important relationships in a child's life—the bonds with parents and other caregivers—maximally respectful of that child's unique character, interests, and potential as a human being. These first relationships serve as important models throughout the child's life for trusting others and forming strong and supportive social bonds, the behaviors from which gratitude grows.

 STRATEGY 7: Help children understand their own and other people's emotions and mental states by having give-and-take conversations regularly during everyday family interactions.

Having regular conversations with children about their own as well as other people's emotions, thoughts, or beliefs is beneficial for promoting children's cognitive and emotional development. Children's comprehension of gratitude by age five is stronger if they have a better understanding of emotional and mental states. Thus, another strategy is to engage children in give-and-take conversations by age three or four that are appropriate to their level of maturity. Such conversations support children's emotional competence as well as their *theory of mind*—the ability to understand people as mental beings with thoughts and motives of their own.

Theory of mind is used to explain to others what one thinks or feels and to interpret what others think and feel. It starts developing by age four and is present in most five-year-olds. It supports perspective-taking, empathy, and more satisfying social interactions with others, enabling children to appreciate other people's kindness toward them and, in turn, to know how to be kind to other people. Developmentally, it's a critical part of gratitude and generosity.

You See Where I'm Coming From

Theory of mind is an important precursor to gratitude because it enables one to appreciate the positive intentions and motivations of benefactors. Without theory of mind, a child wouldn't be able to grasp the personal meaning of other people's kind acts. To illustrate, Jeff's mother-in-law, who his kids call "Mema," gave his then two-year-old daughter, Julianne, cute brown socks with hearts on them as a Valentine's Day gift. Because Julianne was too young to have developed theory of mind, she focused with delight on what she liked about the socks (the color, the details) and automatically said, "Thank you, Mema, I love them" because it was the nice thing to do. But if Julianne had theory of mind she would've eventually understood that Mema gave her that particular gift because she knew brown is her favorite color and she loves her. In this instance, Julianne might have provided a more heartfelt, "Thank you, Mema, they're pretty and you got them in my favorite color!" because she appreciated Mema's intentional act of love.

Fun Is a Lovely Language

Research shows that language plays an important role in developing theory of mind and that simply talking about mental and emotional states with children early on seems to help that development. Talking together during family activities and interactions is critical because language mostly develops as the child internalizes experiences from everyday life. Humans are inherently social animals, and family interactions provide structure and lots of cues that help children process and naturally understand social experiences. The strategies we've covered support the healthy practice of mature discussions *and* interactions, which together strengthen the bonds between adults and children.

When we have lots of conversations with children about the events in their lives and follow their lead by being an active listener and participating in the conversations they want to have, we learn the topics important to them. We'll show later how this helps children discover their skills, develop a competent sense of self, and, eventually, find a sense of purpose.

Take Me to the Zoo, Please

One day, Jeff's then four-year-old son, James, told his father, "Hey Dad, I'd like to go to the zoo." Though Jeff could have responded, "Sounds good, man" and carried on with the day, he decided to be curious about James's specific interests.

"What kind of animals do you really want to see?" said Jeff.

"Lions and elephants," James said beaming.

Had Jeff gone on autopilot, he would've planned a family trip to the zoo they typically visit, and James would've seen the polar bear, snow monkey, and tamandua for the umpteenth time, but no big cats or pachyderms. Instead, aiming to learn about what excites James—and what he might be really grateful for experiencing—Jeff decided that the family was headed to another zoo, one where the lions roam and the elephants graze.

While there, Jeff saw James's love for learning in action. At each and every exhibit, James wanted Jeff to read all of the information presented to visitors. Together, they learned that male lions have thick manes to protect them during fights; that Asian elephants live in herds that average twenty animals; and that collared lemurs like to hang out with hissing cockroaches (bet you never knew that!). With each fascinating new detail, James discovered what he liked, what was gross or scary, what was amusing or touching. At one point, James turned to Jeff and said, "Thanks for taking us to the zoo. I can't wait to tell my teacher about it." As you can see, this example also illustrates how mature give-and-take conversations between adults and children go hand in hand naturally with social interactions, sensitive responsiveness, and autonomy supportiveness in families.

Love Binds Us Forever

Daily discussion of the emotions and mental states of other people is important for helping children develop emotional competence and theory of mind. When significant events occur in a family member or friend's life, parents could ask their child what she thinks the relative or friend is feeling and how she might feel if the same thing happened to her. Such social interaction is critical because it infuses emotions into conversations, sometimes sheer joy and love, as the next example shows.

Consider how Giacomo's son Alex reminded his family to be grateful for the love that they share. From the time he was born, Alex was happiest when people interacted with him. It never ceased to amaze everyone how much he'd remember things and repeat them in his own special way. This was especially true for his "Nonno" and "Nonna" (Giacomo's dad and mom, who took care of him a lot at a young age). Alex regularly dazzled them such as when he'd say phrases in a blend of English and Italian. He was a tremendous source of happiness for his grandparents during a very important time. Giacomo's father was very ill, and Alex—with his long wavy locks, mature interactions and quirky conversations—was a golden gift from God. He brought laughter and delight, tender love and joy, and deep comfort to Nonno and Nonna. And they showered him with love for it. For at least the last two years of Nonno's life, Alex brought more gratitude to everyone in the extended family. Why *more* gratitude? Because that was the emotion everyone clung to regularly during that time to connect, make sense of things, share love, and stand strong through the end.

Through the drama of life's ups and downs, regular discussions and social interactions do much more than help children learn emotions and mental states. They help build meaning in people's lives, young and old, and they help build loving bonds between family members. While gratitude is often felt in the hearts and minds of adults during significant moments in life, it's the emotional support and loving bonds that need to be in place first for gratitude to really start growing in the hearts and minds of young children.

Families That Play Together Find Strengths and Gratitude Together

Discussion and social interaction come together naturally through play, and play provides regular opportunities to make children grateful, too. Families that play together build strong bonds and memories. Parents not only learn to appreciate the uniqueness of a child, but they get a break from the stresses of life and a boost in their own well-being. Hiking, biking, playing board games, or reading books together build up children's self-esteem and help them develop a unique vision of the world and their place in it.

These kinds of play experiences are more important than ever. Schools are squeezing out play and social interaction to make room for "learning," and kids' lives are getting overcrowded by commercial messages and unhealthy doses of isolated, idle screen time. The importance of social interaction during play cannot be underestimated. It's not only a great way to discover children's interests, but their character strengths as well. Character strengths are fulfilling, intrinsically valuable traits nurtured by society and institutions. Once adults know children's strengths and interests, they can engage in mutually rewarding activities, be responsive, and share emotions. Such synchrony improves children's ability to regulate their own behavior and the quality of their parents' relationships with them. Again, caring interactions and bonds provide fertile soil for gratitude to take root.

Interacting during Play and Reading Is Serious Business

Sometimes it can really help to participate in children's play. And that brings us to the power of sociodramatic play. One time, Giacomo's son Alex was playing in his room and he called out for help. When Giacomo came to his call, he explained that he was having trouble suspending a blanket over his bunk bed so that he could keep it dark to help his baby doll fall asleep. Giacomo was just about to weigh the blanket down with some pillows so that he could get back to work. But he followed Alex into the kitchen and watched as Alex reached for a cupboard. Perplexed, Giacomo asked his son what he was looking for. At that moment, Alex fished out a clip from a bag of chips, and Giacomo realized what was going on. Alex had a better solution than he did. It turns out that he had learned that trick from playing with Nonna. Experiences such as these allowed his parents to discover his emerging character strengths of love, kindness, and social intelligence—strengths nurtured by the constant love showered on him during his early years—as he took care of his baby doll.

Appreciating Alex's resourcefulness, Giacomo followed him back to his room and joined in on the fun, saying he'd play the handyman. Alex loved that, and the two talked about details for how he wanted the blanket placed. The handyman explained the best way to clip the blanket to the comforter. There still was a problem, though. They needed at least two more clips. So the handyman went and found two more clips and came back to finish the job. As he put up the third clip, Alex hugged his dad's leg and said warmly, "Thank you, daddy." Giacomo helped Alex achieve his goal of caring for his baby, and, to Giacomo's humble surprise, his son, at the tender age of four and a half, seemed genuinely grateful.

Reading books together is an easy form of engaging play that can be interactive too. The pictures and simple plot lines of children's books make it easy for adults and children to discuss emotional and mental states. Adults can have children elaborate on stories by asking about their favorite character, illustration, or part, and this can spur discussion about children's likes and dislikes, beliefs, and thoughts—all of which stimulate language and reading skills overall. Adults can also discuss the emotions and thoughts of characters in books to bring more fascinating interactions into play.

Any Curious George book is full of such opportunities. If George accidentally lets the penguins loose, for instance, you could pause and ask your child, "How does that make the zoo keeper feel?" and "Why?" Your child's answer and the ensuing conversation may surprise you. That's what happened when Giacomo read a Curious George book to his six-year-old son Dario. He said the zoo keeper would be "Worried." Intrigued, Giacomo then asked, "Why?" "Because he doesn't want the penguins to eat people's food. That will scare them," Dario replied. It was then that Giacomo realized this was an aspect of his son's emerging character strength of *social intelligence*—the ability to perceive and understand others' emotions. Rather than passively reading to his son, Giacomo decided to take a more active role and found an opportunity to connect with him. Doing so not only brought them closer, but it gave Giacomo more insights into the development of Dario's character strengths. Knowing your child's character strengths is important for making them grateful.

 STRATEGY 8: Be a role model of thanking and giving for children. Encourage them to thank, give, and be thoughtful toward friends, particularly using their character strengths.

Children learn about themselves and the world as well as how to behave through observing and imitating others. Although there are many ways to develop into happy and successful adults, the one thing most developmental scholars will agree on is that the path to thriving begins with forging positive social relationships that support one's strengths. Thus, strategy 8 is about showing children how to express thanks and be generous—two critical behaviors for forging gratefulness and supportive social relations—and about how to encourage children to use their strengths in doing so. Generosity and gratitude are intimately tied by being on opposite sides of the coin of beneficial social exchanges. Being generous not only strengthens relationships with others, which promotes gratitude, but the more children give to others the more they'll learn about what it takes to be kind to others and the more they can appreciate kindness in return.

Evidence That Parents Can Make Kids Grateful

We base this strategy on research we're now conducting with two of Jeff's doctoral students, Meagan Muller and Tara Lomas. The research started as a doctoral dissertation by another student of Jeff's, Sara Levenson. We're finding that parents who practice and value grateful expression in their lives have very grateful children and adolescents. Further, parents who reinforce youth for expressing gratitude can also help to make grateful kids.

What I See Is What You Get

Kids are sponges, taking more in from their environment than we often realize. Sometimes this is good, such as when siblings express affection toward each other because their parents are always hugging. Sometimes this is bad, such as when they curse thanks to a potty-mouthed relative. But when it comes to making your kid grateful, one of the most powerful strategies you can use is to frequently express thanks to others and ensure they see it. You could also say prayers of thanksgiving as a family. Though this is an expression of thanks as part of a spiritual relationship, this is another way to demonstrate thankfulness that generally strengthens the valuing of gratitude as well.

Jeff and his wife work full-time, so they need childcare during the week. Fortunately for them, the year their son James was born, friends of the family opened their own small day care in a neighboring town. It was an extension of home, and James was constantly nurtured and showered with love there. To show his appreciation, every so often Jeff would bring his friends their morning coffee. One day, when James was three, Jeff helped him fix his Lightning McQueen puzzle. When this was done, James went to his play diner and brought Jeff a cup of coffee, saying, "Thank you." At first, Jeff didn't understand why James would bring him coffee as an expression of thanks. But soon thereafter, he realized that James was simply imitating his dad who, in his experience, gave people coffee when he was grateful.

Appreciate Even the Things People "Should" Do

Aside from expressing thanks to others, you should also express thanks to your kids. Doing so acknowledges their kindness and shows them that you value and appreciate their efforts to improve your life. This reinforces them for behaving kindly, thus increasing the chances that they'll behave this way in the future. So when your child brings his plate to the sink after dinner, it's in everyone's best interest for you to say a quick, "Thanks, honey."

A common response from some parents, teachers, and journalists we hear is, "Why should I thank my child for listening to me? I'm their parent. Shouldn't they just do as I say?" That's a great attitude if you want to model ingratitude. But if you're trying to raise a grateful kid, is it really that harmful to thank them for things they "should" do? We think not. You would probably thank your husband for taking more home responsibilities so you can meet a work deadline (though he "should," because that's what loving, supportive spouses do, right?). And you would probably thank a friend for giving up her Pilates class to discuss family turmoil over coffee (though she "should," because you recently gave up Bible study to help her move, right?). So just as you would thank your husband or friend in these situations, why can't you thank your daughter for playing nicely with her sibling, completing her homework with little arguing, or going to bed on time? You can. In fact, we think you should.

Be Generous, Be Grateful

Generosity, the act of giving without expecting anything in return, is another behavior to model for kids if we want them to become more grateful. Caring for others is uplifting because it lets us feel like we're useful and making a real difference to people. And it helps us feel like we belong to a caring community, which our research shows promotes gratitude in kids. The more selfless we are willingly, the more we create tight bonds and opportunities to be graced with goodness in return. The generous acts we model for our kids need not always be momentous, such as being the class parent or PTA president. Little acts work fine too. Jeff is frequently a lector at his church's youth rock Mass because it's a small way for him to support his parish and the community's youth. Imitating their dad's service, his kids now enjoy helping with the collection.

Being generous is also something you can do together as a family. Jeff and James enjoy helping their church with their annual carnival, and now Jeff and his family help the "peanut butter and jelly gang"—a volunteer group that can make over a thousand PB&J sandwiches during one meeting for less-fortunate people. Since James started becoming more involved with his church, he's said to Jeff several times, "We're so lucky we have a good church." It's amazing how the simple acts of collecting money during mass, selling cookies at a carnival, and making sandwiches has made James feel like he's part of something important and larger than himself. And it's this very realization that has helped him become more grateful for the blessings he's been given, which in this case is a community vested in his welfare. With such supportive social ties in place, opportunities for feeling grateful and expressing thanks start to grow naturally in the context of children's social experiences.

There are many ways adults can help children be generous on their own. For example, parents could have their kids decide which toys they no longer play with or which clothes no longer fit them and then donate those items to local families in need. Encouraging generosity closer to home, such as toward neighbors or friends, teaches children about appreciation and the value of community. When kids volunteer to help collect the mail or take out the trash for a neighbor, babysit or dog-sit for a friend of the family, or assist a classmate with their homework, they learn about the effort it takes to be kind to others and see firsthand how their kindness is appreciated. Usually though, such kind acts tend to become reciprocated so that a child eventually discovers that building community feels good and helps make life better for everyone. Thus, it's a good idea to not only encourage such generous acts in children but to praise and thank them for such behaviors afterward.

Using Your Strengths to Do Good Deeds

A good strategy for making your child's generosity more genuine and effective is for them to use their character strengths while being helpful to others. We provide a list of the character strengths and their definitions on pages 54–56. You can help your child identify her top strengths by having her take the VIA Youth Survey, for ages ten to seventeen. It takes about fifteen minutes to complete and is free online at www.viame.org. If, however, your child is between the ages of five and ten, you can take the survey for them. If you do this, be sure to cautiously interpret the ranking of the strengths, keeping in mind that the survey wasn't designed for this use. But it works for the purposes of getting a general sense of your kid's strengths.

TABLE 1: *The VIA Classification of Character Strengths*

1. WISDOM AND KNOWLEDGE—Cognitive strengths that entail the acquisition and use of knowledge

- **CREATIVITY** [originality, ingenuity]: Thinking of novel and productive ways to conceptualize and do things; includes artistic achievement but is not limited to it

- **CURIOSITY** [interest, novelty-seeking, openness to experience]: Taking an interest in ongoing experience for its own sake; finding subjects and topics fascinating; exploring and discovering

- **JUDGMENT** [critical thinking]: Thinking things through and examining them from all sides; not jumping to conclusions; being able to change one's mind in light of evidence; weighing all evidence fairly

- **LOVE OF LEARNING**: Mastering new skills, topics, and bodies of knowledge, whether on one's own or formally; obviously related to the strength of curiosity but goes beyond it to describe the tendency to add systematically to what one knows

- **PERSPECTIVE** [wisdom]: Being able to provide wise counsel to others; having ways of looking at the world that make sense to oneself and to other people

2. COURAGE—Emotional strengths that involve the exercise of will to accomplish goals in the face of opposition, external or internal

- **BRAVERY** [valor]: Not shrinking from threat, challenge, difficulty, or pain; speaking up for what is right even if there is opposition; acting on convictions even if unpopular; includes physical bravery but is not limited to it

- **PERSEVERANCE** [persistence, industriousness]: Finishing what one starts; persisting in a course of action in spite of obstacles; "getting it out the door"; taking pleasure in completing tasks

- **HONESTY** [authenticity, integrity]: Speaking the truth but more broadly presenting oneself in a genuine way and acting in a sincere way; being without pretense; taking responsibility for one's feelings and actions
- **ZEST** [vitality, enthusiasm, vigor, energy]: Approaching life with excitement and energy; not doing things halfway or halfheartedly; living life as an adventure; feeling alive and activated

3. HUMANITY—Interpersonal strengths that involve tending and befriending others

- **LOVE**: Valuing close relations with others, in particular those in which sharing and caring are reciprocated; being close to people
- **KINDNESS** [generosity, nurturance, care, compassion, altruistic love, "niceness"]: Doing favors and good deeds for others; helping them; taking care of them
- **SOCIAL INTELLIGENCE** [emotional intelligence, personal intelligence]: Being aware of the motives and feelings of other people and oneself; knowing what to do to fit into different social situations; knowing what makes other people tick

4. JUSTICE—Civic strengths that underlie healthy community life

- **TEAMWORK** [citizenship, social responsibility, loyalty]: Working well as a member of a group or team; being loyal to the group; doing one's share
- **FAIRNESS**: Treating all people the same according to notions of fairness and justice; not letting personal feelings bias decisions about others; giving everyone a fair chance.
- **LEADERSHIP**: Encouraging a group of which one is a member to get things done and at the time maintain time good relations within the group; organizing group activities and seeing that they happen.

5. TEMPERANCE—Strengths that protect against excess

- **FORGIVENESS**: Forgiving those who have done wrong; accepting the shortcomings of others; giving people a second chance; not being vengeful

- **HUMILITY**: Letting one's accomplishments speak for themselves; not regarding oneself as more special than one is

- **PRUDENCE**: Being careful about one's choices; not taking undue risks; not saying or doing things that might later be regretted

- **SELF-REGULATION** [self-control]: Regulating what one feels and does; being disciplined; controlling one's appetites and emotions

6. TRANSCENDENCE—Strengths that forge connections to the larger universe and provide meaning

- **APPRECIATION OF BEAUTY AND EXCELLENCE** [awe, wonder, elevation]: Noticing and appreciating beauty, excellence, and/or skilled performance in various domains of life, from nature to art to mathematics to science to everyday experience

- **GRATITUDE**: Being aware of and thankful for the good things that happen; taking time to express thanks

- **HOPE** [optimism, future-mindedness, future orientation]: Expecting the best in the future and working to achieve it; believing that a good future is something that can be brought about

- **HUMOR** [playfulness]: Liking to laugh and tease; bringing smiles to other people; seeing the light side; making (not necessarily telling) jokes

- **SPIRITUALITY** [faith, purpose]: Having coherent beliefs about the higher purpose and meaning of the universe; knowing where one fits within the larger scheme; having beliefs about the meaning of life that shape conduct and provide comfort

Once you've identified your child's top strengths, hang the results somewhere so you can remember and use them often. When working as a school psychologist, Jeff would have children complete the survey and then tell them to place the outcomes prominently on their refrigerator for all to see. It's worthwhile to brainstorm ideas about how kids might apply their strengths too. Using strengths helps children have more positive social experiences and opportunities to feel grateful.

For example, one teen Jeff worked with was strong in kindness—defined as being generous, nurturing, compassionate, and high in altruistic love and "niceness." Knowing that doing favors and good deeds for others fosters kindness, Jeff suggested that the student regularly visit the elderly in her community. In just a few weeks, Jeff, the teen, and others in her life noticed that her generosity started to spread beyond the elderly and to other groups needing care—such as animals at a local shelter or siblings needing help with homework.

Encourage Kids to Be Thoughtful with Friends

Throughout life, most gratitude and generosity is practiced and experienced in the context of close relationships. Being considerate of the needs of peers and friends is an excellent way for young children to start finding others they can be close to. The sooner this occurs the sooner these natural sources of gratitude are introduced into children's lives. Consideration can be incorporated into everyday circumstances, from inviting friends over on a hot day to play in the sprinklers or to go swimming to finding out what a friend's favorite cereal is and buying it when the friend sleeps over. Regardless of the act, the more in tune a child is to his friend's needs and interests, the more the friendship will be strengthened because of the gratitude generated by his thoughtfulness and the reciprocity that will likely result.

This pattern became apparent with Giacomo's son Dario when he was seven. In the month leading up to his eighth birthday, his mother asked Dario if he wanted to help plan the upcoming party and asked whom he wanted to invite. Dario seemed uninterested. But the next day he came up with a good idea: he wanted a party with a Star Wars theme, something he knew his friends would enjoy. Upon deciding this, Dario "owned" the party planning. Dario excitedly typed up a guest list and another list to keep track of every single party detail, including the decor and food. He started offering suggestions for making the event fun for his guests. When he suggested soda for the party, his mother reminded him he didn't like soda. "It's not for me, silly," he said, "but for my friends. They'd love it if there was soda." He continued, "Also, I want to invite both friends and family to the party because I want them to meet each other." Imagining things his friends would love to do and things they'd appreciate, he wanted to craft a "totally awesome" experience for them.

He and his mother found lots of ideas and resources for Star Wars–themed activities and decorations. And with each idea that he picked, his anticipation grew. The day before the party, Dario helped his parents with the preparations by arranging Lego Star Wars bingo cards—his friends also loved Legos—and he helped make "cool" C-3PO water bottles. The whole family pitched in to construct duct tape light sabers of various colors for his friends to choose from, and he stuffed goodie bags with Chewbacca pencils and Jedi candy. The party was already meaningful, and it hadn't happened yet.

Throughout the planning, Dario used his strengths in many ways. With his autonomy supported, Dario's strengths poured out one by one. His love of learning was evident as he sought to improve his new skill of typing, and he showed creativity with his attention to details that would suit his friends for the crafts and activities. He chose a theme that he loved and knew his friends did too. Plus, he wanted to bring his friends and family members together so everyone would enjoy the party more. These behaviors used strengths of love, kindness, and social intelligence. All of this left his parents awed and created anticipation and savoring all around.

Though the party was a big hit with his friends and with the family, the real surprise—at least for Dario's parents—happened in the few months following the party. Dario was playing more with the friends who had come to the party. One day when some friends were visiting, Dario provided them with snacks and drinks on his own, and, when they left, gave them candies that he knew were their favorites—much to his mom and dad's delight. Giacomo and his wife realized how naturally generosity flows when close friends are involved, how far a little thoughtfulness can go toward creating such friends, and how important it is to use character strengths when being kind and thoughtful toward others.

The bottom line is this: a balanced mix of love and support from adults helps grow authentic generosity and gratitude, thoughtfulness and connection with others, and good times and memories. They all go hand in hand naturally—from the beginning.

CHAPTER 3

Growing Gratitude One Goal at a Time

*H*UMANS NEVER stay still. From the first days of life, curious interaction with the world propels us to use what we know to learn new things. Famous developmental psychologist Jean Piaget regarded this activity as a major force driving the development of our thinking. Humans are problem solvers, always moving from one challenge to the next. In this chapter, we consider how adults can harness this inherent tendency in children and adolescents as a way of fostering in them appreciation and gratitude.

Problem solving and gratitude go together naturally, and each is an essential characteristic of a confident and positive person. Adolescence is a time when identity rapidly takes shape in ways that will affect one's course in life significantly. We researched how gratitude develops in adolescence by following more than four hundred kids ages ten to fourteen for four years, and we identified four basic patterns of gratitude development:

* *Thrivers* entered their teen years with a moderate amount of gratitude that increased.
* *Deficients* entered their teen years with low gratitude that remained low.
* *Squanderers* started out with a high sense of gratitude that decreased.
* *Late Bloomers* started with a low sense of gratitude that increased. (See figure in notes.)

The general picture emerging from this ongoing research is that with gratitude comes other adaptive behaviors that help people succeed. In the fourth and final year of our longitudinal study, we discovered that Thrivers had many more qualities associated with personal responsibility and "good character" than Deficients. For example, Thrivers, compared with Deficients, reported more self-awareness, self-respect, optimism, and confidence in their skills to succeed at tasks—qualities of individuals who feel mastery over their skills and responsibility for adhering to personal standards. But Thrivers didn't just feel more confident and personally responsible than Deficients. They also reported more goals, self-control, intentional self-regulation (or the ability to regulate themselves to achieve goals), and plans for the future—all characteristics that help individuals reach higher standards. Consequently, grateful teens were also more involved in extracurricular activities and possessed more social assets like role models and caring teachers who support their goals. It's no surprise then that Thrivers also had more vitality (alertness, energy, and enthusiasm) than Deficients.

We hope that this snapshot is enough to convince you why gratitude and goal-directed behavior complement each other well in kids. This brings us to our next strategy; encouraging personal responsibility and providing effective guidance as children hone their skills and interests.

STRATEGY 9: Help children learn appreciation through personal responsibility by giving them encouragement and realistic support for their efforts and achievements as well as by teaching them to accept the consequences of their decisions.

Before children reach adolescence, there is the serious business of play that promotes their cognitive, emotional, and social development. Play allows us to bond with children in memorable and developmentally crucial ways. *Scaffolding*, the word psychologists use to describe the assistance older members of a culture give a child until the child becomes independent in a new behavior, characterizes how most parents play with their young children. Individualized support like this brings about more mature behavior in children as they become socialized. To see how scaffolding builds up skills let's consider how Giacomo uses it with his eight-year-old son Dario at the park.

Scaffolding Achievement during Play

Imagine the specific steps involved in playing Frisbee. Letting go of the Frisbee just before it's aligned with a target is important for throwing it in the proper direction, for example. This can take a while to learn because several steps and muscles must be coordinated (turn the torso, swivel the hips, move the arms and wrists). Giacomo supports the execution of each step by demonstrating part of the task, explaining the steps, simplifying difficult parts, or giving reminders—all common forms of scaffolding.

When helping a child to learn a new task, though, the devil is in the details. The more quickly an adult helps a child reach some noticeable degree of success, the more the child will stay encouraged. With confidence will come less anxiety, greater focus, and improvement. As progress builds, it helps to point out that progress and provide encouragement for the effort a child puts into it. Ideally, the activity should become a rewarding experience for both parties. That's what happened during one Frisbee session with Dario. But it came after failed attempts, frustrations, and angry fits. So before describing the rewarding experience at the end, let's consider some of the challenges along the way because, no matter what the activity is, children will fail, and when they do they may doubt their ability.

For this reason, it's critical for adults to be observant of the specific behaviors a child needs to adjust to execute a step or series of steps.

Though it's difficult to watch, it's important to let kids try new things and fail because that's part of the learning process. And we owe it to them to provide honest feedback about what doesn't work and why. They won't always accept it, or it may hurt their feelings—especially if they're sensitive to criticism. But if we always tell our kids how good they are at activities, without being realistic, we're just giving them a false sense of confidence that can be crushed when they're put to the test.

Kids aren't always open to help, and sometimes they reject it outright. When Dario threw the Frisbee way off to the side, rather than listen to his dad's advice, he threw it harder and failed again—a cycle he repeated until he got the Frisbee stuck in a tree and huffed, "Oh forget it, I stink." Defeated, he wanted to go home and just call it a loss. Fortunately, Giacomo was able to knock the Frisbee down, but this time he wasn't able to convince Dario to try again. Young children can be confident in their abilities even though they aren't realistic in assessing them, which destines them to frustration and disappointment. So, when do we step back and let this ride—and when should we help? This is the balance you have to figure out as a parent. Your kids may eventually tire of failed strategies and become open to your advice. Sometimes, however, it may be better left to try on another occasion after they've cooled down.

On another trip to the park, Frisbee went better. The last decisive step Dario needed to throw accurately was flicking his wrist and releasing his fingers right after, something he learned by throwing first at a close distance. It didn't take long after he got the throwing part down that he improved his catching, too. In fact, in quick succession, Giacomo and Dario worked together from positioning the arms to snatching the Frisbee and from anticipating the trajectory of a throw to keeping the knees nimble in case a quick jump was needed because of wobbles due to wind. Soon both were in the zone playing progressively better, extending the distance between each other and picking up the pace. Dario would throw fast accurate ones, to which his dad exclaimed, "Laser!" and Giacomo would spin himself around before throwing a crazy curve, which Dario caught with ease. The pride on Dario's face was clear, as was the gratitude in his heart. On the way home, Dario said to Giacomo, "Thanks for teaching me to play Frisbee. I love it! Can we play more when we get home?"

When No Help Is Better than Some

A child's developmental stage and actual aspiration must be considered when deciding how much to support her and when to let her do it on their own. Jeff and his wife, Cara, try hard to support their three-and-a-half-year-old daughter's aspiration of being the best mommy she can be to her baby dolls. Part of being the best mommy is changing their clothes frequently. When Julianne first started playing mommy with her dolls, Jeff and Cara were constantly changing the doll's clothes for Julianne because she didn't know how. But, with patience, practice, and fine-motor skill development, Julianne started changing her doll's clothes independently. While Julianne's minitantrums caused by frustration could have been avoided had her parents just kept doing this chore for her, it would've robbed Julianne of a chance to improve her skills and gain autonomy—essential for a well-adjusted and grateful child.

This kind of support—one where you're as hands-on as needed in the beginning to one where you let go enough for them to own the activity—helps children discover their interests, and it builds their skills and confidence in tackling challenges. It also gives them a sense of responsibility for the outcomes of these activities, something adults can encourage in kids. Gaining personal responsibility teaches children to value certain activities and skills, and this gives them things to appreciate.

Helping kids learn new skills is a great way to build real, not just superficial, confidence that, in turn, encourages them to try other things. As children learn to labor for activities they love, they gain appreciation for those activities and their skills, and this enables them to feel grateful when helped. The more children have valued activities and skills in their life, the easier it is for other people to see them doing what they love and to support them in those areas—and this invites more gratitude.

Scaffolding Academic Achievement

If your child is genuinely confused about what to do on an assignment, first ask what he thinks is required. Here's where scaffolding comes in handy. Are there misunderstandings you can clarify? Can you explain things in simpler terms? Can you suggest ideas to get him started? Better yet, can you brainstorm together? Once he has grasped the task, leave him to it. If he gets stuck, step back in and offer support to move him along. Be encouraging along the way. But don't do his work. Once he's finished, check for major errors, explain why those parts are incorrect, and have him redo the work until it's correct.

Learning isn't always smooth, though. For example, while our oldest boys (Giacomo's son Dario and Jeff's son, James) both love reading and learning, they've each gotten into trouble for not doing their homework when they were supposed to. Rather than completing their work, they were playing on an iPad or a Kindle. And when we took the devices away and asked them to finish their homework, they protested how "unfair" we were being or how much they "hate homework." Giacomo, frustrated one day after Dario had stormed to his room and slammed the door over this, called Jeff and learned that the same problem had just happened with James. It turned out that Dario needed a break from what was admittedly a long task, and James just wanted a little longer break than usual after just getting home from school. During stressful moments like this, it's tough to get kids back on track immediately. Putting your child in timeout or giving him another consequence (i.e., taking their nighttime show away) might be an appropriate response, depending on the situation. But importantly, during such trying times parents must also figure out why their child misbehaved so homework gets completed next time with less difficulty.

Setbacks are part of learning. Good rules help kids through, and this kind of support over time also promotes gratitude. When we help kids learn from their mistakes or bad choices and they behave better next time, this shows that they're appreciating our advice and taking responsibility to do their best. It's easy to think during stressful moments with kids that they don't appreciate what we do for them. Gratitude, however, grows as kids make improvements because of our help. But be careful. We can sometimes help our kids too much.

Lend One Hand, Not Two

It's all too easy for parents to get sucked into doing too much for their children. You may have heard the term *helicopter parents* before. It's when parents micromanage children, a phenomenon that increased with the advent of cell phones.

You may think that helicopter parenting doesn't apply to you. But here's a form of it that can easily happen to anybody. Your child, crying out with frustration and despair while doing homework, proclaims that he "just doesn't get it" or that he "can't do it," and you step in because you care about his learning and want to help. Or—let's be honest—maybe you're just tired of the whining. But, by the time you figure things out, you find yourself writing down the details about what lead to the Punic Wars and how the Roman Empire emerged as a dominant power—all while your child looks on, content with the progress. Don't get sucked into this! It's good to support your child, but doing the work for them does more harm than good.

Think about it. If you always jump right in to help a child when she's struggling, how will she ever build the skills and confidence to succeed? Butterflies can spread their wings only after they struggle and break through the cocoon. The same applies to children. If we want them to soar, they must fight for it first—and endure some tears, bumps, and pain along the way.

A common complaint adults make is that "kids these days are handed everything and don't appreciate anything." Indeed, one survey found that two-thirds of parents said they were concerned with their children's sense of entitlement. So are kids today becoming more entitled? According to research by Jean Twenge and Keith Campbell, the answer is yes. They report in their book, *The Narcissism Epidemic: Living in the Age of Entitlement*, that entitlement recently increased by 30 percent in just a fifteen-year period in children, adolescents, and young adults. With entitlement comes the attitude that "people owe me something" or "I deserve this" or "great things should come to me." These attitudes are very self-focused, making people forget about the kindness they've received from their benefactors, thus giving them little reason to feel grateful. They also interfere with children achieving their goals because they instill a passive approach to achievement rather than the active one we are suggesting here.

Adults can turn the tide and start countering this sense of entitlement by providing children with regular opportunities to grow personal responsibility, which will help them take ownership of good outcomes and make them less inclined to feel cheated when they don't get their way. No achievement will make a child grateful if she thinks she has a right to everything.

The Importance of Personal Responsibility

Rosalind Chow, assistant professor of organizational behavior at the Tepper School of Business at Carnegie Mellon University, and Brian Lowery, professor of organizational behavior, Graduate School of Business at Stanford University, conducted an experiment in which they gave people an allegedly difficult achievement test and a chance to win some money for doing well. They then provided them with a helpful hint. Here's what they found: everyone regarded the hint as helpful, but only those who felt personally responsible for the achievement score felt grateful for the hint; those who felt their score didn't reflect their effort didn't feel grateful for the hint. Until this study, gratitude research had focused exclusively on external attributions for benefits. That is, when people feel that others are responsible for benefiting their welfare they feel grateful toward those people. Chow and Lowery showed that if people are to feel grateful for help they receive, they must also feel personal responsibility for their achievements.

Just as it's important for kids to feel a sense of personal responsibility for their achievements, it's equally important for them to feel the same for their mistakes and learn to live with the consequences of their decisions. So if your teenager decides to sleep in instead of going hiking with neighbors and then gets upset that he's missing out on the fun when he decides to get up, resist the urge to drive him to the trails. This teaches responsibility and helps him become self-reliant and autonomous. We choose our behaviors. But we can't choose our consequences, nor can we escape them.

Love Leads to Learning

Encouraging kids to do things independently, give their best effort, and live with the consequences helps build their self-confidence and sense of personal responsibility for their actions. This is how kids come to care about and appreciate things in life. And when peers understand what matters to them and mentors help them in these areas that they value, they'll be grateful.

Supporting and encouraging kids' activities—by providing guidance and honest feedback on what went well and what didn't and then working with them on specific steps to improve—gives them skills for achieving goals and confidence. Would you feel proud of a good dinner you made for friends if it was ready-made? No. But, would you if you prepared it from scratch? Yes. Accomplishments are sweeter when we're personally invested in them from start to finish. When we praise kids for their achievements, show our delight, and support the effort they put into the process each and every time—regardless if the outcome is successful or not—our response rewards them for trying to do new things and encourages them to trust their skills and keep trying. The more kids feel that others believe in them and their potential, the more they will believe that they have qualities of value and the more they will be motivated to build up those qualities. Love in this form helps kids discover and develop their abilities and interests. Over time, kids will feel grateful by learning to appreciate all of the people who supported their achievements, and, in turn, they'll learn to support others in similar ways. Gratitude will then grow more and more in your kids' lives—and in the lives of everyone involved with them.

 STRATEGY 10: Help children develop self-control and authenticity by framing obstacles as challenges and opportunities for growth.

Ten-year-old Melissa came home from school with a big smile on her face, grasping her perfect math quiz for everybody to see. Her mom, delighted by all this, said that she was so proud of her. Her aunt, who happened to be there, exclaimed, "You're such a smart girl!" Mom takes the quiz from Melissa, pins it up on fridge, and adds, "Let's put this here so everyone can see how intelligent you are." Most people would find this scene heart-warming. Parents and adults commonly praise children's academic success by saying they're "smart." But it turns out that this kind of praise can hinder children's academic motivation and success.

Carol Dweck, Lewis and Virginia Eaton Professor of Psychology at Stanford University, has studied motivation and achievement in children for decades and recently discovered that there are two basic types of people: those with a *fixed mindset* and those with a *growth mindset*. People with fixed mindsets believe that human qualities—such as intelligence, talents, and abilities—are carved in stone and that everybody is born with predetermined levels of these qualities that cannot be changed, regardless of effort. For them, failure always directly reflects people's competence and worth and is debilitating when they encounter it. By contrast, people with a growth mindset believe that human qualities can be cultivated through effort and that everybody can change their potential by applying themselves and gaining certain experiences. For them, failure is a challenge, an opportunity to learn and improve. Cultivating a growth mindset is key if adults are to help children learn from their mistakes and grow over the long term. The more kids are open to this process, the more they can appreciate the investments others make in them and, in turn, attract more benefactors.

Having a growth mindset produces very real results. For instance, psychologists from Stanford University and Columbia University examined how a fixed mindset versus a growth mindset influenced the academic performance and motivation of junior high school students. The transition from elementary school to junior high can be difficult for many students. Performance standards become higher, classwork gets harder, and personal attention from teachers diminishes for students. In one study, the researchers followed 373 seventh graders for two years. While all the students may have found the transition to junior high challenging, not all of the students' math grades suffered equally. Only the students with fixed mindsets showed an immediate and steady decline in math grades over the two years. Further, though both groups' math grades were comparable in elementary school, it was only the students with growth mindsets who pulled ahead during junior high.

To see if a growth mindset was actually responsible for this academic advantage, the researchers then tested if teaching students a growth mindset helped. They randomly assigned about one hundred seventh graders who were struggling academically to either an experimental or control workshop, which lasted eight weeks upon entering junior high. Both groups received instruction on study skills. But the experimental group read an article, "You Can Grow Your Intelligence," and discussed how neural connections in the brain grow stronger when new material is learned. The control group read an article about memory and discussed ways to remember new information.

The results were staggering. Not only did the growth mindset training help shift students toward believing they could grow their intelligence, but it produced greater motivation (as observed from teachers) and improved grades in math from the spring of sixth grade to the spring of seventh grade. Before this study, most people believed that intelligence was set for life. This research, however, shows that we can become smarter by simply *believing* we can become smarter. How does this tie into making grateful kids? Again, we believe that the more children are open to growth opportunities, the more receptive they'll be to other people's investments in them, and the more they'll attract benefactors in the future—giving them more reasons to be grateful. Moreover, the same way children can learn to become smarter, they can learn to become more grateful. Gratitude, like intelligence, is not fixed. There's always room for growth.

Praise Process, Not Outcomes

When adults praise a good performance as being due to intelligence or some inherent trait, as was the case with Melissa, they encourage children to achieve for the sake of getting high grades or looking smart rather than the goal of learning or improving. This is problematic when children fail because they won't know how to cope with that outcome. They'll begin to doubt themselves and decide that they're not so good or smart. This can occur not only with schoolwork but with athletic and creative achievements, too.

The message such praise sends is that adults value kids *because* of their intelligence or their talent. It tells kids that adults' love is conditional—"they love me when I get an A on a quiz, hit a home run, or land the lead role in a play"—rather than uncondition-al—"they love me *regardless* of my grades, athletic performance, or acting ability." Accepting the message that one is "smart," "athletic," or "talented" by nature makes kids shy away from challenges or from trying to improve their skills because they run the risk of realizing that they aren't the smart or talented person they or others thought they were. They'll believe they're admired and loved for winning but disliked and rejected for losing. Worse, a child for whom good grades come easily may even come to believe that she doesn't need to put much effort into her studies. This child sets out into the world believing in her talent but is unprepared in any real sense for the future. A child whose sense of personal success is rooted in having figured out how to take a test and get a good score is ill-prepared to enter the work world, where the rules—and the stakes—change and performance is evaluated very differently.

Parents who want to acknowledge the beloved qualities of their child must also encourage the child's efforts to strengthen those qualities. Praise the effort that goes into the learning process. If a child formulates a new strategy or different approach to solve a problem or asks lots of questions about new material he's learning in school, praise those specific behaviors. The important message such praise sends is that success requires hard work. The result is that children will likely work harder in the future. And when they eventually do encounter failure, rather than break down over it or avoid it to feel positive, they'll confront it, look to see what they did wrong specifically, and—perhaps—ask what they could improve. Encourage effort but avoid undue pressure to succeed because the anxiety your child could experience will overwhelm the potential for growth. Instill a growth mindset in your kids so that they develop qualities that they and other people can appreciate and want to improve. That's how most individuals actually succeed in the world, as those of us who watch reality TV from time to time know. We are touched to see youth who've pushed their talents to the limits and consequently express overflowing gratitude to the mentors who believed in them and encouraged them to dream bigger.

The more kids are aware of their abilities and care to improve, the more they appreciate it when others help. When a child strives to improve himself, it's easier for others to see him as a worthy investment because they'll trust that he'll make full use of their help. We know this firsthand as professors because we enjoy giving our time and effort to students who want to grow. Doing this makes us, and our students, feel grateful.

Protecting Kids' Authenticity

Efforts to open kids up to confronting challenges and wanting to grow will only do so much for making them grateful, though, if environments are counterproductive to developing good character. The media environment of today's youth offers a diet high in commercial messages. Media is meant to entertain and feed commercial interests. Therefore, media often portrays unrealistic views of how people should be (glamorous, violent, dramatic, extremely successful), making kids believe that they'll be accepted and happy if they pursue these unrealistic and unhealthy standards rather than be authentic. *Authenticity*—living in accordance with one's values and beliefs in most situations—is related with higher self-esteem, life satisfaction, and more positive emotions, in addition to less stress, anxiety, and negative emotions.

Gratitude and being authentic are complementary; they focus individuals on the essentials in their lives, helping them to appreciate themselves and be fulfilled with what they have. Helping kids believe in their hearts that they're complete and okay as they are and teaching them to be critical consumers of media messages will help them stay motivated to push themselves and achieve goals that are valuable for their future and society.

Not only is much of the media content misleading, but it also threatens to crowd out and discourage the kind of growth experiences necessary for success and gratitude. Unfortunately, many kids today are duped by these messages. They buy into the notion that sheer desire for prized qualities is enough to make them successful. And with the Internet, this may even happen sometimes (e.g., posting a video or blog entry that goes viral). But it's rare. And importantly, identifying strongly with media messages can distract kids from getting to know their strengths and pursuing the more realistic goals of improving their skills and acquiring the requisite experiences and opportunities that make happiness and success happen.

The truth is that good character and success come from love of learning, hard work, learning from failure, and more hard work. We'll say more about the media in later chapters. For now, it's worth noting that thriving involves knowing your strengths and skills and surrounding yourself with opportunities and people who enable you to improve yourself and aid others—all things that help create gratitude.

Support Your Child's Plan for Success

There are ways to help a child frame and approach large tasks so he's motivated to do his best. Here we draw on the research of Edwin Locke, Dean's Professor Emeritus of Leadership and Motivation at the University of Maryland, College Park, and Gary Latham, Secretary of State Professor of Organizational Effectiveness at the Rotman School of Management, University of Toronto, whose theory of smart goals is widely used to improve employee motivation and performance. *Smart goals* are: (1) clear, specific, and measurable; (2) challenging but attainable; and (3) self-set and committed to. The first feature provides structured benchmarks that focus adolescents' attention on goal-relevant activity that's easy for them or an adult to monitor. The second feature makes objectives realistic enough to actually achieve but hard enough to be personally rewarding when they're reached. And the third feature energizes ownership of the plan.

Teens tend to rush into things and fail to appreciate the importance of planning. Let's say your teenage daughter decides she wants to make honor roll. Without a plan, it's possible she might become discouraged if she stumbles and give up entirely. You can help her set smart goals to drive her motivation and creativity by: (1) suggesting specific and measurable goals such as taking good notes in class and summarizing the main points at the end of each day; (2) encouraging her to keep goals realistic and stay organized by creating a checklist; and (3) advising her to join a study group to make it easier for her to commit to her aim. Helping her set goals in such detail will empower her and help her succeed. It will also open her up to even greater opportunities to feel grateful.

Self-Control for Self-Improvement

Developing gratitude and self-control go hand in hand. Florida State University Frances Eppes Scholar and eminent psychologist Roy Baumeister and his colleagues have found that an individual's self-control acts like a muscle. It takes effort to use and depletes willpower in the short run. In the long run, however, the more self-control an individual exercises in one area of life the more likely he or she is able to develop it in other areas.

Angela Duckworth and Martin Seligman, faculty at the University of Pennsylvania's Positive Psychology Center, show how important it is to have self-control. They measured eighth graders' ability for self-control through questionnaires completed by the students, their parents, and their teachers and through a task in which students had the option to receive $1 immediately or $2 if they waited until the end of a week. Over the course of a year, they found that students who had high self-control also had better attendance and standardized test scores. They were also more likely to get into a competitive high school program. But perhaps the most significant finding of the Duckworth-Seligman study was their discovery that self-control is a potent predictor of academic success—better than the students' IQ!

Even more powerful evidence of the value of self-control comes from the Dunedin Multidisciplinary Health and Development Study in New Zealand conducted by Terrie Moffitt, a professor from Duke University. Moffitt and her colleagues tracked 1,037 individuals from birth to age thirty-two to examine their self-control and health. After controlling for differences in socioeconomic status and general intelligence, the researchers found that individuals with high self-control (again, measured through questionnaires completed by the children, their parents, and their teachers) grew into adults who had better physical and mental health, fewer problems with substance-abuse and crime, were more responsible with money, and were generally financially secure. Self-control, therefore, appears to be an important key for consistently improving life, while the lack of self-control leads to greater dysfunction.

When it comes to goals and gratitude, then, each aspiration reached helps a child dream of—and plan for—more out of life. The more a child wants to improve, the more he'll gravitate to people who will value and contribute to this growth. As a result, the child embarks on a road filled with opportunities to appreciate help. The more children stay true to themselves and grow from experiences like this, the more positive they will be about the world, passing on this drive to grow to others. This is how gratitude blooms in children and spreads in society.

 STRATEGY 11: Use management strategies to help your children organize their responsibilities and follow through on their commitments.

The Challenges of Parenting Today: The Work-Life Balance

Parents across the world grumble about the challenges of parenting. It makes sense given the fact that an increasing number of homes across the industrialized world have both parents working. More than ever, it's critical for parents and kids to get on the same page and figure out ways to achieve their respective goals. This gets harder to do as kids grow up and start juggling more responsibilities. Thus, strategy 11 gives you tools to help organize life for your family members—and yourself.

A research project carried out by Ellen Galinsky, president and cofounder of the Families and Work Institute, gives us clues about where to begin. Using a nationally representative sample of 1,023 children, ages eight to eighteen, and their 605 employed parents, Galinsky began her study by asking the children one question: "If you were granted one wish that would change the way that your mother's (or father's) work affects your life, what would that wish be?" Adults were asked to guess their children's answer; the results were intriguing. Most parents (56 percent) guessed that their kids would wish for more time with them, but only 10 percent of kids wished that for their mom, and 16 percent wished that for their dad. More kids wished for their parents to be less stressed and tired, 34 percent for moms and 28 percent for dads. And only 2 percent of parents guessed this! Galinsky's results also showed that children felt more positive about how they were parented when they spent more time with their parents. Recall that a parent's consistent availability forges a child's secure attachment and trust. It makes sense, then, that parents' simply spending more time with their kids helps them feel more positive about how they're being raised.

It appears, however, that the quality of time is what seems to matter more to kids. How does more "quality time" with children help them achieve their goals and increase their gratitude? To answer this, let's consider the late Stephen Covey's *law of the harvest*. Suppose you're a farmer, Covey writes, and you want to reap your harvest of corn in the fall. What must you do? Can you hang out all spring and summer and sip iced tea while watching your dog chase chickens? No way. You must first prep your soil so that it's nutrient-rich, moisture-retentive, and well-draining. You must then prepare rows of soil so that you can sow the seeds properly. Afterward, you must water the plants regularly and protect them from weeds. Tending to your crop brings on fall's bounty.

Just as you can't force corn to grow without cultivating it, you can't properly support your child's commitments and goal-strivings unless you *consistently* spend quality time with them. Not only do kids want more quality time with parents, they *need* it. *Parenting* is a verb because it describes an action. We think most parents would agree when we say that raising kids is hard, and raising kids to be their best is the hardest thing you'll ever do. This requires self-management, which will help you be a principle-centered parent, someone who remains committed to the goal of raising a grateful child by putting first things first, to use another of Covey's life principles.

Management tools can help maintain this attitude of being your own master. The goal here is to fulfill work and other responsibilities while also protecting the sanctity of your family time so that you can be present consistently to help your children with their goals, ultimately making them more grateful.

Get Members of the Family on the Same Page through Family Management

We've talked with many parents about ways they address conflicts and nudge their kids to be more responsible. By no stretch of the imagination are their homes, or ours, stress-free palaces of peace. But one thing is clear: families that use tools to manage life at home seem to enjoy better relationships with kids, compared to families who don't. Common tools for success include checklists and responsibility charts. Kids love them because checklists and charts provide a clear and organized approach to manage many tasks, which is particularly important as kids age and take on more responsibilities independently. Aside from reinforcing cooperation and responsibility in kids, such management tools also reduce stress in the home, helping family members bond—all ingredients for making grateful kids.

The checklist and responsibility chart methods came in handy in these ways once when Giacomo's wife was sick with the flu. Giacomo sought out his kids' assistance to "help get things done so Mom could feel better." Alex emptied the buckets of trash from the different rooms into the kitchen trash bin; Dario cleaned up and vacuumed the living room; and each child dragged his dirty laundry to the washing machine. Both boys then helped set the table together. Thanks to their management system, the division of labor was clear and everything got completed quickly. Dinner that evening was special for everyone, and the whimper of "thank you" that Mom extended afterward was as sweet as the reward his kids received for being so responsible.

Of course, our kids don't spend all of their time at home with mom or dad, so it's equally important to extend support to them as they venture out to work and play with others outside the home.

 STRATEGY 12: Provide a community of practice for children so they learn to adapt to challenges and achieve goals together with others.

We've explained how management tools help support movement toward goals and the development of a growth mindset, which both promote gratitude. But kids rarely strive for goals in isolation; they also rely on help from others. In truth, the most important goals in a young person's life will be identified outside of the home. And let's face it, parents may never be able to motivate their children to achieve as much as others can. Young people are constantly assessing their abilities and the development of their skills in comparison to their peers. A crucial way parents and other adults help children achieve and become more grateful is by providing them with opportunities to work on goals shared with others.

Involving Children in Group Activities in the Community

When groups of people share interest in a craft or activity and improve their skills as they interact regularly, they all develop themselves in a supportive community. Sports and hobbies often provide kids with such *communities of practice* outside of the home. External environments, especially those involving activities the child chooses, become more and more influential as the child ages.

The goals kids set in such environments can be very powerful and motivating.

Giacomo and his wife saw this unfold with Dario and his karate lessons. They hoped that karate lessons would help Dario gain physical and athletic confidence—and he did. Nothing could take Dario's focus off the new moves he was learning, and the sound of his "kiai's" regularly reverberated throughout the house. The community of practice he had entered—the instruction and feedback from the sensei and the mentors, the examples set by other students, and the rules of respect and perseverance in the dojo—taught him the importance of goals and self-discipline for succeeding and improving himself, whether he was in the dojo, at home, or at school. Unlike other activities or sports he'd been involved in (soccer, baseball, Cub Scouts), this was one he really valued. He talked about it with friends, showed moves to peers at school, and demonstrated his skills to his younger brother, Alex.

When it came time for Dario to test for the yellow belt, he did whatever it took to advance to the next level. As the test approached, his persistence was clear as he practiced regularly and described with enthusiasm the moves he needed to perfect. Unlike other goals his parents had helped him with, this goal was all his. When he passed the test, the whole family savored the moment by going to Dario's favorite restaurant and talking about what he liked most about karate.

Finding activities a child loves, especially if they're in the context of a community, is a great way to make him open up and mature. Emblematic of Dario's budding self-confidence, thanks to karate, was this quartz crystal necklace that he started wearing as his style became more "cool." He made more friends, and, to his excitement, some boys invited him to join their club at school. Consequently, Dario learned to appreciate a new sport and the community support and encouragement he received. He also realized that good relationships, be they with mentors like his sensei or friends, are valuable sources of gratitude.

Team sports and organized clubs like the Boy Scouts or Girl Scouts provide lots of opportunities for kids to cooperate with others, help others, receive help, push themselves to do better and succeed—all experiences that promote gratitude, generosity, and character. Jeff's son James, for example, participated in a holiday cake-baking contest for Cub Scouts. The Scouts were very creative making cakes that ranged from Frosty the Snowman to the entire nativity scene, lambs and all. When the contest ended, each Scout was responsible for giving the cakes to community members such as firefighters, nuns, and nursing home residents. Jeff and the other parents watched their sons' faces light up when the person receiving the cake responded with a heartfelt, "Thank you." Not only did the boys feel good for surprising someone with a cake, but they felt extremely grateful for connecting with the people in their community because they felt valued and appreciated.

How does all of this relate to making grateful kids? Genuine gratitude occurs once individuals start having a story of their own—of achievements and challenges they've faced—and communities of people that value them and what matters most to them. It's community, inside and outside the home, that helps kids identify and build up their strengths. And such experiences create a motivation to not just become more authentic and better—partly because it's a way of expressing thanks to the people who've invested in them—but to pass the favor on to others and to society in their own unique way too.

This notion that a community of practice could inspire gratitude in youth and help them reach new heights was evident in the amazing story of the 2013 Westmont College women's basketball team in

Santa Barbara, California. Coach Kirsten Moore had always been selfless with her team members, but little did she know how this would come back to her. In May 2012, her husband died unexpectedly when she was eight months pregnant with their first child. Her husband's wish was that she never let his illness stop her from chasing her dreams, and that's just what she did. As the new basketball season began that August, the grieving widow and single mother, still shaky from grief, stood before the team and presented the players with a challenge. It was going to be hard, she told them, but she had to do this, and they had to join her on the difficult journey.

The team of mostly average players stepped up to the challenge, winning twenty-four of the twenty-seven regular season games. Along the way, friends from the college and from Moore's neighborhood helped by watching her baby and lending emotional support to help her and the team keep going. The night before the NAIA national championship game, Coach Moore realized that the season hadn't been just about winning or losing basketball games. She said, "It was about a test of the human spirit, and we had passed that test, and accomplished something bigger than ourselves." Right through to that last championship game, the players on the team were with her 100 percent; throughout the sweat and tears of the season, they pushed themselves like never before, and they achieved the dream of a national title.

What motivated everyone to work together and try harder than ever to beat the odds? This community took on the grief and misfortune of one family as their own. Inspired by the story of courage and perseverance embodied by their coach, the players collectively accepted the challenge to become the best team they could. In the end, they thanked their coach with the supreme victory, and their coach was tearfully thankful in return. They surprised themselves by what they achieved and saw life flowing vigorously through each of themselves and through Moore's baby, Alexis. A new story was born for this community, as they each came to see themselves in a new light.

This inspiring story shows what's possible when people work together against challenges, and it shows how gratitude and goals can grow from even the steepest terrain to help individuals blossom into the best people they can be.

CHAPTER 4

Building Strengths and Resilience
by Staying Positive and Learning to Cope

*J*N MANY WAYS, Jessica was a typical teen in a high school where Jeff worked at as a psychologist. But she was far from typical when it came to academics. She was ranked eighth in her class during her junior year, putting her in great shape to apply to the University of North Carolina—her first choice for college. Then misfortune struck.

While playing soccer she severely injured her knee, tearing her MCL, ACL, and meniscus. During her recuperation, she became extremely sick and was diagnosed with Type 1 diabetes. Jessica thought to herself, "I blew out my knee, and now I have to deal with being a diabetic. Can anything else go wrong?" Believe it or not, one more bad turn awaited her. One picturesque afternoon, Jessica was abducted at gunpoint in the middle of town; she escaped, but barely. As you can imagine, Jessica needed a lot of support, at home and at school, to cope with everything that had happened to her in such a short time. Jeff started seeing her regularly for counseling and worked closely with her family and an outside therapist. During one session, Jeff asked her, "What's your secret? Most people would've fallen apart, withdrawn from the world, and totally given up. But here you are, only a few months after everything, and you're still in a great place mentally, emotionally, and academically."

Jessica's response blew Jeff away: "Aside from having an amazing family, teammates, and friends who've been there for me every step of the way," Jessica said, "I realize that it could've been a hundred times worse. I know this may sound weird, but I'm actually very grateful. I'm very lucky to be here today in the shape that I'm in. But I know I have a tough road ahead of me."

Any one of these experiences would've been enough to leave most adults—let alone teens—defeated, but Jessica stayed positive and seemed clear about the challenges ahead. Even more remarkable, she was grateful. Not only was gratitude empowering her to keep going, but it had helped her mature. She realized how all her hard work and all the efforts of the people who helped her were almost wasted. The fact that she was still in a good position to use her strengths and move forward with her plans made her extremely grateful despite the string of bad events. This energized Jessica, eventually getting her accepted at the University of North Carolina.

Jessica's story illustrates that gratitude serves us well, especially when times are bad. Youth, however, must first build up their confidence and self-esteem as a reserve for weathering such times, and parents and other adults can help with this. In chapter 2 we discussed the importance of discovering your kids' character strengths as a prerequisite to their learning gratitude. Here, we offer a blueprint for how to connect kids to a positive view of their life story so that more authentic gratitude can take root. This includes a discussion of how to put character strengths to use more, emphasizing their role in helping children acquire competence, a sense of belonging, and autonomy—all fundamental human needs.

Character strengths are the virtuous qualities that people use to have meaningful, fulfilling experiences in life. About ten years ago, Martin Seligman and his colleague, the late Christopher Peterson, led a team of research psychologists in creating a classification manual of human character strengths and virtues. After reading everything from the Bible to Pokémon cards, the researchers determined that there were twenty-four universal human character strengths, such as kindness, courage, and humility (see Table 1 in chapter two for a list of all character strengths).

We're born with the capacity to excel in all of the strengths. But most of us become high in some strengths and low in others thanks to nature and nurture. As a parent, *you* have the power to nurture your kid's strengths. Jeff's father, for example, has an intense love for nature, and he did everything possible for Jeff to develop this love as a child. As an adult, Jeff has a keen appreciation for the beauty of nature; for example, each fall he chooses one tree to watch for daily, subtle changes in the color of the leaves.

Research shows that developing certain character strengths can make one more satisfied with life, especially strengths of the heart, like gratitude. Further, students who set personally meaningful goals *and* use their character strengths in new ways become more hopeful and engaged in school. We've already learned how to discover kids' strengths; so we now turn to our next strategy: helping kids use their strengths creatively so that they acquire the social and emotional reserves to become individuals who can weather all storms.

 STRATEGY 13: Encourage children to use their character strengths creatively to meet the fundamental human needs of competence, a sense of belonging, and autonomy.

According to self-determination theory, all humans share three innate needs that drive their motivation, personality development, and well-being: (1) *competence,* a drive to affect one's environment and achieve valued outcomes within it; (2) *a sense of belonging,* the drive to feel connected to others; and (3) *autonomy*, the drive to engage in self-selected behaviors concordant with one's strengths and personality. Not surprisingly, psychologists call these *fundamental human needs* because one must satisfy these needs for a fulfilling, happy life.

As a human strength, gratitude undergirds our capacity to fulfill all three fundamental needs. A virtue of transcendence, gratitude connects us to entities and meanings greater than ourselves and clears the path to achieving our unique and coherent life stories.

The Importance of Fulfilling Fundamental Human Needs

Having and valuing intrinsic goals—such as affiliation, growth, and community—improves mental health and well-being because they help people fulfill their fundamental human needs of competence, sense of belonging, and autonomy. On the other hand, having and valuing extrinsic goals—such as wealth, fame, and image—harms mental health and well-being because they don't help fulfill those fundamental needs.

For example, say a teenager skipped soccer practice to work more hours at his job because he wanted to save up for a new pair of flashy rims for his car and look cool. Rather than sharpening his skills and coordination with teammates, he worked into the night delivering pizzas. The consequences for this poor decision are much greater than you might think. To start, he missed an opportunity to learn new drills and possibly become a better soccer player while also missing out on the experience of getting energized with his teammates for an upcoming championship game against archrivals. And because he missed practice and didn't learn the new plays, his coach made him sit on the sidelines during the game. The game came down to the wire, with his team just clinching the win. While his teammates basked in the glory with the entire school roaring, he felt disconnected and regretful. Though he was a little closer to his goal of sweetening his ride with some new rims, he was robbed of a chance to feel good about himself and grateful for achieving a major goal with his teammates. Thus, pursuing extrinsic goals and neglecting intrinsic goals cost him an opportunity to fulfill his fundamental human needs—and increased his gratitude.

Using Strengths to Achieve the Goals That Matter

Making grateful kids means teaching them to value intrinsic goals, such as affiliating with teammates on a valued activity and growing the skills to succeed and be recognized by a community. It also means teaching them to put less of a premium on external measures of accomplishment—or extrinsic goals—such as making money to acquire fancy items for peers to recognize and admire. We also want our children to succeed in pursuits that are in line with their intrinsic goals. We can do this by strategically helping them use their character strengths.

Jeff's son, James, is an excellent reader. He's loved books from day one. Toddler Julianne loves books too—so much so that Jeff and his wife sometimes find it hard to do their household chores because Julianne constantly wants them to read to her. One day, Jeff and his wife realized that James could read to Julianne. It would be a great opportunity for James to use his top strengths (i.e., love of learning, an ability to love and be loved, and kindness) to connect to Julianne and personally grow. Jeff discussed the idea with James, and, before he could finish speaking, James excitedly said, "Yeah, I want do it!"

Immediately, Jeff and his wife saw the effect that reading to Julianne had on James. His sense of competence increased, as he's passionate about helping others learn new things, and reading to Julianne helps him achieve this goal. His sense of belonging sky-rocketed, as he loves this special time with Julianne and feels closer to her than ever. And his sense of autonomy strengthened because he personally decided to read to his sister and enjoys helping out his parents. This activity completely played to James's strengths and personality. Using one's strengths to fulfill essential human needs is a superb way to make kids grateful because it allows them to have more rewarding social experiences. It also builds up their social, emotional, and mental reserves, which they can then tap into during rough times.

Distraction Can Cost You Fundamental Connections with Your Child

Raising grateful children by helping them use their strengths affects how deeply parents are able to bond with their children and under-stand what makes them tick. When work, volunteer commitments, or social pursuits demand our time, it's all too easy to become dis-tracted when our kids ask for our undivided attention. One of the biggest obstacles to learning about your child's unique strength pro-file is being distracted, and being distracted definitely impacts how you raise your child.

We've all been guilty of letting our kids play video games or watch television to keep them busy while we return e-mails, wash dishes, or organize a special event. Giacomo sometimes tries to be every-thing to everyone and ends up having to settle for less playtime with his kids. It's all too easy to overextend ourselves and be distracted by things outside the home, but it should be taken seriously if it regularly affects kids.

Distractions rob you of the energy and attention necessary to really get to know your children, their dreams, concerns, strengths, and weaknesses. In other words, distractions take away opportunities to learn about your child's developing sense of self. Recall from the last chapter that children want more quality time with parents. If you can be mindful and focused on your child, then you're more likely to learn about what he or she is good at, thus giving you a more rewarding parenting experience and giving your child a better chance at using their character strengths to achieve intrinsic goals and, therefore, become grateful. Let's be more specific about the importance of fulfilling fundamental human needs in our children's lives.

 STRATEGY 14: Help children focus on areas that matter to their self-esteem, and help them appreciate the good people and good experiences in those areas.

Help Children Recognize Their Benefactors

Children evaluate their competencies in domains that matter to them. Specifically, they evaluate their scholastic competence, social acceptance, physical appearance, athletic abilities, and behavioral conduct. These impressions then become integrated into an overall self-evaluation, or sense of self-esteem.

Adults learn about a child's sense of his or her specific competencies in each of these domains by having two-way conversations with their child. Such conversations help children begin to identify their qualities and behaviors responsible for making them feel the way they do about themselves; from there, children piece together their sense of self-esteem. These conversations also help you learn who else has had a positive influence on your child's life. For instance, you may learn that your daughter now has a vicious corner kick because her soccer coach gave her some extra one-on-one instruction. You may learn that your son now understands the solar system better thanks to a friend who gave up some recesses to tutor him.

Once Giacomo found his son Dario typing out a report about red-eyed tree frogs and asked him about it. Dario replied, "My teacher gave me this cool book about amphibians. She wants to know which animals are my favorite and why. So I'm going to give her this report." As Dario finished the report Giacomo asked him to add a little thank-you note because it was nice of the teacher to give Dario a book about something he liked learning about. He was happy to oblige. After you have identified benefactors in a child's life responsible for bolstering his competence and self-esteem, you should share this insight with the child so he knows who to be grateful to and why. Some kids may do this themselves, but a gentle reminder from you won't hurt anyone, and it can only strengthen those special bonds.

By early adolescence, kids' self-esteem becomes influenced more by interpersonal relationships. Domains such as romantic appeal and quality of close friendships become central to how adolescents feel about themselves. Accordingly, adults can identify the positive elements in an adolescent's social life. Who's helped them during challenges this week? Who accepts them just the way they are? Who pushes them to reach their potential? As teens become more aware of the caring and supportive people in their lives, not only will they feel better about themselves in general, but they will also feel more grateful.

I Think I Can, I Think I Can!

Self-efficacy, the belief in one's ability to succeed in specific situations, creates the basis for a child's self-esteem. Self-efficacy plays a major role in how one approaches goals, tasks, and challenges. Indeed, it has a particularly strong effect on people's motivations.

Higher self-efficacy helps people take a broader view of a task, facilitating their ability to problem-solve and dig deeper to achieve goals when they encounter obstacles. Generally speaking, with high self-efficacy, people are more likely to put forth a lot of effort for an extended period of time to complete a task. In contrast, people with low self-efficacy believe they'll perform poorly and view difficult tasks as things to be avoided. Pointing out to your child the relationship between his blossoming self-efficacy and the coaching he has received from teachers and friends is another step in helping him become grateful.

A special quality of gratitude is that it stems from and supports individuals in improving themselves and gaining greater self-efficacy. Take a moment to think about areas in which you are exceptional. Maybe it's that you can make a three-course meal for twenty guests without breaking a sweat; maybe you can whip together a knockout presentation for work in hours; or maybe you can still spike a volleyball better than that smug twenty-year-old you just played. To excel at any of these tasks, you have not only put in your time, but you also had to face and beat obstacles along the way. You probably didn't do it alone. Just like thinking about the benefactors who helped you achieve your high level of competence makes you grateful, the same goes for your kids. Helping youth recognize the role that others have in teaching them skills and helping them problem solve their way to success is a great way for making them grateful.

Self-Efficacy and Small Improvements: Keys to Staggering Results

Recall the story of Giacomo's son Dario getting his yellow belt in karate? Confident in his stamina from all the practice he had put in and pumped up from the momentum of his achievement, Dario set his sights on another athletic goal: the PTA fund-raising run. With his parents' encouragement, Dario eagerly sought sponsorships from family and friends for the race. On race day, he went to school sporting his quartz necklace and ready to devastate.

Sure enough, when his mom picked him up at the end of the day, Dario was proud and excited. He had run more laps than anyone in his class, and staff and peers had congratulated him. As a reward, he and the other winners were treated to a special McDonald's lunch with the principal, and the principal thanked them for helping raise money for the school. Later that day Giacomo asked how that made him feel. "It felt good to help the school," Dario replied, and his gratitude was evident when he added that he was happy the principal noticed his hard work.

Those two events created a larger pattern for Dario. The momentum also spread to other areas, and his tenacity increased in soccer and basketball. His parents even noticed a dip in his complaints that he was "no good." Eventually, Dario chose to compete in a karate tournament (not something everybody elects to do), and he placed third. We provide this example to point out that parents can promote self-efficacy in kids by encouraging them to take opportunities, like the race—to make small improvements in a set of valued skills. This will help the child garner more support and consequently more gratitude for their achievements and that support.

Such opportunities are ideally matched to kids' interests and are slightly above their ability level to produce more *flow experiences*. Flow experiences occur when one uses a high level of skills in highly challenging tasks. Having a flow experience boosts confidence in one or more domains and pushes a child to try harder and gain strategies to improve his skill. That's how flow experiences push individuals toward personal growth. Indeed, our research shows that adolescents who experience flow are not just grateful, but they tend to thrive and want to make a difference in the world.

Using Strengths to Bolster Self-Esteem and Self-Efficacy

We know that kids are more likely to develop a positive sense of competence and selfhood when they're regularly engaged in challenging activities that are meaningful to them. Enhance your kids' experience and increase their self-esteem and self-efficacy by helping them use their strengths during such activities. Create a mutually reinforcing cycle by challenging kids to apply their top strengths in new ways in areas that matter to them. This increases their chances of succeeding and feeling good about themselves and the people who helped them. The more this occurs in a child's life, the richer that child's life story will be and the deeper the gratitude.

Let's turn to an example to illustrate. Debbie was a twelve-year-old middle school student Jeff saw regularly for counseling. She was extremely bright but suffered so badly from major depression that she cut her wrists several times. The emotional damage she experienced was devastating. Jeff often consulted with her outside psychologist and psychiatrist to ensure everyone was on the same page, but no matter what medication or therapy technique Debbie tried, she remained very depressed. She was an expert at telling people she was a failure. When asked to describe her assets, she'd quickly say, "Nothing. I can't do anything right."

Jeff asked Debbie to complete the strengths survey discussed in chapter 2 to identify her strengths. Given her emotional state, she wanted nothing to do with "taking another stupid test," but with a little patience and persistence she reluctantly agreed to complete the survey. Her top three strengths turned out to be love, kindness, and a love of learning. Simply knowing that she had a set of important strengths put a little smile on Debbie's face, however briefly. It would take much more than learning about her strengths to help Debbie with her depression, poor self-worth, and self-defeating beliefs, so Jeff and Debbie brainstormed together ways she could use her strengths.

Debbie was a master at origami. She could twist a piece of paper into a fire-breathing dragon in under a minute. So Jeff asked her if she'd be willing to teach origami to Frank, a student he saw who also liked arts and crafts and was having trouble connecting with other kids at school. This, Jeff thought, would let her exercise all of her top strengths. Love would be used because, although she was currently depressed, she valued close connections to others, and helping Frank could be the basis for a real friendship. Kindness would be used because she enjoyed helping others and taking care of them, and teaching Frank origami would allow him to learn a new artistic craft and show him that another student valued him. She'd use her love of learning because she'd have to master new skills to teach Frank new origami shapes if she was to keep him interested and engaged. Debbie agreed to help Frank. The plan worked! Within a month, Debbie and Frank developed a close bond. It was so close that they'd meet Jeff in his office weekly to have lunch and discuss new and exciting origami designs. Watching this beautiful friendship develop, Jeff met with his assistant principal to discuss another strategy to help Debbie with her depression and get her more invested in herself and schoolwork.

Seeing how successful Debbie was at using her strengths to help others, Jeff suggested that for several periods a week Debbie could be a teacher's helper in a classroom of students with basic academic needs. He argued that not only might this help the other students learn—because Debbie was an honors student and a nonthreatening, easy-going peer—but also that Debbie might gain the confidence and self-esteem she needed to cope with her depression. The assistant principal, who thankfully was willing to do anything for her students, agreed to the plan. And that week, Debbie began assisting the special education teacher. Soon Debbie's parents and teachers began to notice that her mood had lifted. She was participating in class more, conquering challenges instead of being conquered by them, and seemed to have more self-acceptance than ever.

This remarkable story shows how critically important it is for children to learn about what strengths they have and to put those strengths to use. Knowing their strengths and then acting on them gives kids the confidence needed to overcome and cope with even the worst kind of adversity.

Know Yourself and Compare Yourself to Others Wisely

Let's build on what you learned from the last chapter now to see how authenticity and positive social connections contribute to personal development *and* the capacity for gratitude. In part—but only in part—an individual's confidence and self-esteem comes from other people. We compare ourselves to others to develop skills and gauge how we're doing. As kids approach adolescence, they imagine an ideal self, capable of qualities and performances that meet specific standards, which they use to evaluate their "real" self. The degree of discrepancy between the ideal self and real self together with the amount of social support received from peers, parents, and other adults influence the teen's developing self-esteem.

The more in tune kids are with their strengths and talents, the better they're able to set expectations for themselves and thereby navigate social comparisons more effectively. In turn because they will have a better sense of their skill level in areas important to them, they'll choose someone with slightly higher skills as a basis for comparison. Such comparisons are solid ground for teens to take advantage of because they can put into practice strategies they've learned or advice that has been offered by mentors, coaches, exemplary friends, teachers, pastors, or other adults to help them improve and succeed. Consequently, they'll better meet their fundamental human needs of competence, belonging, and autonomy, and they'll have more opportunities to experience and express gratitude.

Let's consider what can happen to confidence, self-esteem, and gratitude for kids who are unaware of their strengths and talents. Such children and adolescents are more haphazard with their social comparisons and have unrealistic ideal selves. They may compare themselves to peers who are more skilled than they can realistically emulate, which produces more discrepancy between their ideal self and their real self and, as a result, leads to disappointment. They may then swing toward comparisons against less-skilled peers to feel better about themselves. Or, worse, they may say or do mean things to certain peers as a way of compensating for any dissatisfaction or insecurity, which socially can then escalate and spread if some peers like and encourage such aggressive behavior. Either way, they're not building skills, confidence, or self-esteem, and they're not meeting their fundamental human needs. Their world is filled with fewer people and things to appreciate. Kids who don't know their strengths and passions make less effective social comparisons, and this invites confusion and dissatisfaction—not fulfillment and gratitude. We're not suggesting that you run your child's social life, but feel free to level with them if necessary.

Supporting Kids When They Are Outshined

Even a teen who knows and uses her strengths will, from time to time, meet another teen significantly more talented than she and may experience this encounter as a crisis. One way to support your child in such a situation is to point to the good people and things associated with all of the areas that matter to her. To a teen distraught that she wasn't nominated prom queen, for example, you might say, "I know how much being prom queen meant to you, and I can totally understand why you're upset." In other words, be validating and nonjudgmental. You could also gently remind her how attractive her boyfriend and everyone else thought she was in her prom dress. Such social support is critical for kids' encouragement as they explore their talents and develop into their own person. And it teaches gratefulness in adversity, which brings us to the next strategy.

 STRATEGY 15: Teach kids to be persistent and see opportunities in adversity. Help them appreciate that their knowledge and self-insight will help them cope with any challenge and that others stand ready to support them.

Modeling Successful Coping

Overcoming a crisis through one's own plans and actions helps youth achieve a strong sense of identity. Kids learn their crisis management skills from observing how their parents and other influential adults cope during emergencies or other hard times.

Before you can help children see adversity as an opportunity for growth or help them appreciate that they can overcome the obstacle, you must help them keep their emotions in check. People don't think clearly when flooded with intense negative emotions. Problem solving goes out the window. That's because negative emotions narrow our thinking and limit the behaviors we use to confront problems. Emotional self-regulation, therefore, is the first coping skill we want to model for our children.

So instead of wigging out because you can't find your daughter's tutu and ballet practice is about to start, take a few deep breaths and tell yourself something like, "Okay, we're probably going to be late and there's nothing I can do about it at this point. I'd love to be on time, but being late isn't the end of the world." Having this more rational, effective attitude will help keep you calm to better think about where the tutu could be. And what do you know? There it is right on the couch where you left it—but under your husband's coat. Damn him!

Emotional regulation is often easier said than done, especially for busy parents. One day Jeff allowed his two kids to sleep later than usual, so things were a little hectic at the breakfast table. The kids were fighting over a jelly bracelet, which Jeff asked them to put down—several times. But before he knew it, his son ripped the bracelet from his daughter's hands, spilling his cereal and milk all over himself. Knowing the bus was arriving shortly, Jeff lost it and barked, "Are you kidding me? I told you several times to stop. Clean up this mess NOW. Don't even think about asking me to watch TV tonight!" While it would have been okay for Jeff's kids to see him get annoyed or even upset, his overreaction wasn't the kind of behavior Jeff wants his children to emulate.

Consistently and successfully regulating your emotions is extremely important for creating a peaceful home and raising happy, healthy, and grateful kids, even though it's hard work. When Jeff was in private practice, he would often have parents write, "learning a new skill takes practice and patience," in their nondominant hand to demonstrate that although something might seem difficult and unnatural at first, with time and continued effort it will become a habit and feel more comfortable. While we personally understand how tough it is to always remain calm when you're trying to multi-task and run a home, we also know it can be done—and you can do it.

Children also imitate parents' positive behaviors when things go bad, as did Janet, whose parents divorced when she was ten. After the divorce, her mother dated infrequently, never having long-term relationships because she wanted to give every minute she had to Janet and her younger sister. Around the time Janet turned seventeen, though, her mother met a man and fell in love. Things were great—at first. Then a relationship initially filled with flowers, nice dinners, and laughter became one filled with anger, jealousy, and tears. Janet's mother stayed in this abusive relationship for a few months. During that time, family, friends, neighbors, and parishioners at her church urged Janet's mother to leave the relationship, but she found that very hard to do. By being persistent, however, in seeking help and social support and praying to God regularly, her mother found the strength within herself to end the relationship.

Soon thereafter, Janet became romantically involved with a boy from school. Although she was extremely hesitant to begin a relationship given her mother's horrible experience, this guy seemed to be everything she wanted in a boyfriend: nice, funny, caring, and cute. The boy-next-door guise quickly faded, and he began to accuse her of cheating, demanding to check her cell phone. He would yell at Janet and tell her she wasn't giving him enough attention. One time he even pushed her. Janet was in an emotional whirlwind. She thought she had found the guy of her dreams. "But if he loved me so much," she thought, "why was he being so mean?"

Janet knew that she, too, would soon be walking around with bruises unless she followed her mother's example and extricated herself from the toxic relationship. She confided in her mother, friends, and guidance counselor and turned to God. Tapping into her social support and love from God, Janet mustered the courage and confidence to tell her boyfriend that the relationship was over. The experiences of Janet and her mother had such an effect on

Janet that when she turned eighteen she began working for a local organization that helped young women in abusive relationships.

Help Kids Use Adversity to Grow

Helping our children become resilient is a great gift we can impart to them, and many of the strategies we're discussing promote resilience. Social skills, confidence, and self-esteem are all qualities that help build resilience, as do close bonds with parents and supportive adults and institutions outside the home. Gratitude also plays a critical role in resilience.

The tragic events of September 11, 2001, gave psychologists a rare opportunity to study factors that may protect people from the emotional damage caused by disaster. Barbara Fredrickson and her colleagues were able to extend a study of a group of adults they'd been following before 9/11 so that they could assess the frequency of positive and negative emotions before and after that tragic event. Frederickson found that of the twenty emotions assessed in the study, gratitude was the second most experienced, after compassion. The people with moderate or more amounts of these and other positive emotions were less likely to experience depression after the terrorist attacks. Gratitude fosters coping, adjustment, and resiliency during bad times with kids as well as adults. An archival review of newspaper accounts about what children were thankful for before and after 9/11 found that themes of gratitude for basic human needs—family, friends, and teachers—increased.

The main reason gratitude is such a potent asset for coping with adversity is because it helps garner social support and piece together meaning when it's needed most. One way to give kids the social support they need during adversity is to help them appreciate the resources they have to cope with a challenge. You might remind them about experiences they've had overcoming similar challenges in the past and discuss how they can use their knowledge from those experiences to handle the current problem. Jeff worked with a teenager who had a mother who was so overwhelmed by her job that she'd often get moody and belligerent. One day, the teen came to Jeff's office crying that she "couldn't take it anymore" and "didn't know what to do." Aside from being emotionally supportive, Jeff reviewed with her the coping strategies she's used before (e.g., listening to music, writing in her journal, going for a walk, calling a friend or relative to talk about something other than her mother) to deal with this situation and navigate her mother's mood swings. Though this didn't prevent her mother from snapping at her, it helped distract the teen so she could survive the ordeal.

Aside from directly supporting your kids, you should also support them in their efforts of surrounding themselves with people outside of the home who genuinely—and reliably—care about them. This is the heart of our next strategy. If we want our kids to be resilient and grow from adversity so that they can become grateful, we must help them build up social, emotional, and psychological reserves. Nurturing their close relationships, taking care of others, and being generous toward others is a necessary step in achieving that goal.

 STRATEGY 16: Teach kids to nurture their close relationships for social support. Help them identify ways to be generous and helpful to others.

Loved ones provide security and social support. Much of who we are and what we've accomplished is because we've been fortunate enough to have been blessed with caring people in our lives. The kinds of relationships we're discussing aren't your three-hundred-plus Facebook "friends." They're the ones who know all about us and love us just the same. They're the ones we can share our darkest, innermost thoughts with knowing that we're accepted unconditionally. Building these kinds of relationships takes time and effort and involves give and take. This strategy will help you guide your child to build the social capital needed to overcome adversity.

While parents play a tremendous role in giving social support to young children, friends begin to take on more of this role as kids enter adolescence; by midadolescence friends are the major providers of social support. One strong clue that having friends plays an important role in children's lives is the research finding that having at least one supportive friend reduces loneliness and victimization for children who are shunned from larger peer groups. Having one or more close friends provides an emotional safety net for children, which gives them a sense of security and helps them cope with major life stressors, such as parental divorce or family discord. Further, close friends promote the social competencies and self-esteem of children from cold and disordered families, suggesting that close friends support resilience.

Make Your Friends a Priority

Parents are by far the most important models in their children's lives. Kids hang on to every word we say and want to copy everything we do. So, if you want your child to have loving, supportive relationships for their own sake and to buoy them during crises, you must show them through *your* actions that having quality friendships is important. This is hard given how hectic life can be.

Consider this scenario. It's 6 a.m. Your kids rise by 7 a.m., sometimes earlier to make your morning routine more interesting. You have one hour to shower, dress, eat breakfast, make lunches, and start a load of laundry. And, hopefully, you have time to mentally review the day—a step you took last week when you remembered to send your son off to school with his leprechaun hat for crazy hat day but not yesterday when you accidentally drove your daughter to day care instead of your mother-in-law's. By the time you get to work, you already feel like you've put in a full day. Your afternoons and weekends are jammed with schoolwork, soccer, karate, swimming, gymnastics, and the Lego club. You're so busy that you don't notice your husband's new, "hip" haircut. You can't possibly make time for your friends.

But you *must* make time for your friends. Doing so will fill your life with the love and companionship in ways that only friends can. It will also make you a better spouse and parent. "Thanks for telling me something I already knew," you may be thinking. But here's another reason why making time for friends is so important, one that you may not have considered: it shows your kids that friends matter and that giving them your time and attention is a wise investment. It's also a balance in your life you want them to see and hopefully imitate someday.

Jeff's friends are some of the biggest blessings in his life. He's been lucky enough to have the same group of friends for over twenty-five years. In high school, naysayers told Jeff and his friends that they wouldn't maintain their friendship through college because everyone went to different schools. Instead of losing touch, they took road trips to each other's schools to visit and hang out. When college was over, everyone once again went their own ways. Some continued with school, others went into business, and still others became firefighters and police officers. But they kept in touch, constantly nurturing their relationships.

Each friend now takes a turn hosting a monthly guy's night, and Jeff and his friend Sal have been meeting for breakfast monthly for the past seven years, missing only once when Jeff's daughter was about to be born. This commitment led Jeff and his friends to be in each other's wedding parties and to be godfathers to each other's kids, who are developing amazing friendships with one another. We know this example is more the exception than the rule, but we share it to let you know that such friendships are possible and can reliably fill your life with gratitude and moments of appreciation.

Jeff's kids see the devotion he has to his friends. They know it's important to be kind, thoughtful, and loving toward friends and others. Sometimes his kids get upset when he's leaving to see his friends; he kneels down, looks them in the eye, and holds them while reminding them that he loves them dearly and that it's very important to make time for friends because "friends are special people." While his children are still young and there may be a sniffle or two after this, through his actions and words, they're starting to understand that having a few close friends is one of life's greatest treasures. And to get the full bounty, one must put first things first and make friends what they should be: a priority.

Teach Generosity and Other-Centeredness

Generosity is the habit of giving without expecting anything in return. For a child, this can be as simple as helping a friend tie his shoelaces, or it can be more involved, like helping a friend learn to ride a bike. The more children are kind to other people, the more they'll learn about what it means to be generous, and they'll also see how others appreciate their kindness.

Parents must set an example of generosity if they want their child or teen to do the same and, consequently, become more grateful. Because they will be around someone who's very helpful (you), your kids will be more primed to think in terms of "who needs help" and more likely to help when they see someone in need. Further, your empathy toward others who've experienced adversity should encourage your children to be empathic and improve others' lives as well.

An experiment by Felix Warneken of Harvard University helps us understand the circumstances under which children will be generous and helpful toward others. Warneken investigated whether children as young as two would help an adult without being asked or if they needed to be prompted by cues. The test was to see if the child would spontaneously help an adult who had dropped something or if the child would only help after being asked. Warneken found that children didn't need to be asked to help, indicating that even toddlers are capable of spontaneous generosity. But are there things adults can do to increase the chances that children will help when others need it?

If you're successful in modeling empathy, you'll start seeing the positive effects in your children when they're very young. Jeff and his wife, for example, are emotional, even mushy at times. Watch the right commercial, and get ready for the floodgates to open. Although they assumed James and Julianne would emulate their parents' behavior, they never imagined how much. When James was two he sobbed like crazy after seeing a commercial about rescuing animals because he thought something bad was going to happen to his dog. When younger daughter Julianne was the same age and was watching the movie *Dumbo*, she became hysterical and began shaking when kids at the circus picked on the little elephant. This is not to say Jeff's kids are only empathic toward animals they see on TV; they're also empathic toward people.

James recently fell, smacked his knee on the ground, and began to cry. Julianne bolted to the freezer, got him his Nemo ice pack for his "boo-boo," and then darted to James's room to get his favorite Captain Underpants book. She then ran over to James, gave him the stuff, hugged and kissed him, and said, "I love you, Jay-Jay. Now you'll feel all better." Though smacking one's knee isn't a major crisis in the grand scheme of things, at the time it was to James. Approaching it the way Julianne did—giving James physical, emotional, and social support—was a wonderful way to strengthen an already magical sibling relationship. Julianne can expect that when she smacks her knee, James will be right there with all the love and affection she needs.

Children don't lose their capacity for empathy when they reach adolescence. Jeff worked with Doug, seventeen, who came from a very loving, other-centered family who tended to each other's needs as well as to those of their community. Doug's family regularly ate dinner together, participated in events on the weekends together, and volunteered at their church for tasks that they could do as a family. One day, Doug found himself in a difficult situation.

He was talking on the phone with Tom, a friend whom he thought he had helped get off drugs not long ago. Doug noticed that Tom's speech seemed slurred. He asked him if he was drunk or high, and Tom admitted that he was using heroin. Appreciate that before this hyperemotional conversation started, Doug was studying for his SATs, which were in a couple of weeks. What should he do? Should he try helping his friend again? Or should he keep studying? Being surrounded by a generous family must have influenced him, because Doug put his own immediate needs aside and rushed to Tom's house.

Once there, he flushed Tom's drugs down the toilet and destroyed his drug paraphernalia. Doug's actions were a turning point for Tom. His road to recovery was tough, but Doug made it easier by supporting Tom every inch of the way. Doug shared with Jeff that Tom's sincere gratitude and thanks was one of the more heartfelt experiences of his life. This touching story illustrates how growth through the good and the bad and support from others make gratitude a central part of every person's unique story on their way to thriving. If your goal, then, is to help your children nurture the important relationships in their lives to give them more reason to be grateful, you should encourage them—through words and actions—to be generous and kind toward others.

CHAPTER 5

Valuing Others Develops Character and Gratitude

*G*RATITUDE NOT ONLY strengthens our relationships, but it also supports our ability to make good moral choices consistency. But it only started getting serious attention from psychologists in 2001. Specifically, Michael McCullough and colleagues proposed that gratitude serves three moral functions. Gratitude acts as a *moral barometer* that helps us assign value to the behavior of others; it acts as a *moral reinforcer* because expressing it increases the chances that benefactors will behave morally toward us again; and it acts as a *moral motivator* because experiencing it causes us to reciprocate kindness to benefactors and extend kindness to others. While these researchers found solid evidence from an array of studies supporting the *barometer* and *reinforcer* functions of gratitude, it wasn't until several years later that researchers produced evidence supporting the *moral motive* function. Together, the three moral functions of gratitude indicate that being grateful tunes us in to valuable interpersonal relationships and helps us reinforce and spread kindness.

All three moral functions of gratitude have one thing in common: being aware of others' kindness enhances our own lives. Giving and receiving are important forms of social interactions that bring us countless advantages. So we wondered, can kids become more grateful by training them to think more deliberately about receiving gifts? In other words, can kids be taught to think gratefully about beneficial social exchanges? Yes.

 STRATEGY 17: Encourage children to recognize the good intentions and sacrifice behind the kindnesses they receive from others and the personal value of such gifts.

Teaching Children How to Think Gratefully

People feel grateful because they think differently compared to those who are less grateful. Gratitude is our acknowledgement that a benefactor intentionally helped us, as well as the recognition that our welfare has been boosted because of the benefactor's kindness. In other words, we experience gratitude because we recognize that we've received something we value that was costly to a benefactor, who intentionally and altruistically provided us with that something. Alex Wood and his colleagues found that people differ in how they habitually viewed interpersonal benefits on these three dimensions—*personal value, intent,* and *cost*—and that this kind of thinking helps explain why grateful people feel grateful.

When Jeff spoke with Alex about this, they started to wonder if people could be made more grateful by teaching them how to think gratefully. Jeff suggested to Katherine Henderson, a doctoral student he was advising, that she use these groundbreaking findings about the nature of gratitude in her dissertation. Katherine agreed and then created a preliminary curriculum designed to teach children ages eight to eleven how to think gratefully.

Using this curriculum, Jeff and Giacomo then brought in other colleagues to more rigorously test it. In one study, five weeks in duration, children were taught either the gratitude curriculum or a control curriculum (i.e., children discussed daily and habitual activities). Children who received the gratitude curriculum showed increases in grateful thinking and gratitude as well as an increase in positive emotions in general, compared with students who received the control curriculum. The gratitude curriculum group maintained the positive effects up to five months later.

In a second study, children received the gratitude curriculum or the control curriculum daily for five consecutive days, rather than weeks. After the curricula were completed we had an opportunity to see if the gratitude curriculum had immediately influenced students' behavior. We asked the teachers who had participated in the experiment, and who were unaware of which curriculum their students had received, to see if the kids would be willing to write thank-you cards to the PTA for a multimedia presentation it had just sponsored. We also asked the teachers to rate their students' happiness on a scale from one to ten before and after administering the curricula.

Children who received the gratitude curriculum reported more grateful thinking and feeling more gratitude, compared with children who received the control curriculum. Further, not only did the teachers rate the children who received the gratitude curriculum to be happier, but those students also wrote 80 percent more thank-you cards to the PTA, compared to the children who received the control curriculum. Thus, the gratitude curriculum brought about changes in the kids that were observable to their teachers and exhibited in their behavior. Teaching children at a very young age how to think gratefully not only can be done, but doing so also boosts children's well-being.

Grateful thinking training doesn't have to take place in the structured forum of a classroom, and we share it with you as a scientifically supported strategy for making grateful kids. You can easily use its basic principles to teach your children how to think gratefully in everyday life. For example, let's say your nine-year-old son, Ricky, is struggling with long division. His friend Brayden skips going to a movie to help Ricky study for an upcoming quiz. Ricky will recognize this was nice of Brayden; kids discern helpful and unhelpful behaviors easily at an early age. But you can help your son build on his recognition and increase his grateful thinking and feelings of gratitude in a brief conversation: "Hey Ricky, that was extremely nice of Brayden to come over and help you study for your math quiz [you're identifying Brayden's intent]. You know he gave up going to see *Rise of the Guardians*, a movie he wanted to see [you're reminding Ricky of the cost to Brayden]. And see, you were getting the long division questions right by the time he left—he seemed to really help you with that [you're showing Ricky the personal value of Brayden's help]. You're a lucky guy to have a friend like that." Teaching children when they're young how to think gratefully this purposefully helps grateful processing become a natural habit for them.

These grateful thinking principles can be applied to expressing thanks to other people. Continuing with the previous example, Ricky's parents can encourage him to thank Brayden while considering these three dimensions of grateful thinking. For example, Ricky might say to Brayden, "Thank you very much for seeing that I was having trouble with division and needed help. I know you really wanted to see *Rise of the Guardians*. It was nice of you to help me instead. Thanks to you I feel like I understand it better." Using these benefit appraisals to guide one's thanking strengthens the overall experience of the beneficial social exchange for everyone involved.

Further, the benefit appraisals can also be used to develop gratitude as part of a child's relationship with God. Beyond thanking Brayden, Ricky could express thanks in prayer more thoughtfully. The more the appraisals guide his thoughts and actions—whether it's toward others or toward God—the end result is the same: he learns to better recognize his good fortune and the goodness of people and God.

What do young children think are moral behaviors? Specifically, what behaviors do they actually do to be generous to others and what behaviors do they appreciate from others? Do girls and boys of different ages have different ideas about generosity and appreciation? Let's see.

 STRATEGY 18: Encourage children to have empathy for other people's feelings and to be kind to others. Teach them to be appreciative when benefactors consider their specific needs.

Out of the Mouths of Babes

We examined how young children identify common acts of appreciation and generosity by asking teachers at a school in Orange County, California, to instruct their students, ages five to ten, to generate examples of helpful or kind behaviors that students their age do. The teachers didn't specify whether students should give examples of appreciation or generosity. We obtained data from 262 elementary students, 116 boys and 146 girls, looking for themes and patterns.

Helping other kids who get injured was a very common theme across all age categories for both generous and appreciated behaviors. *Sharing food with someone* was another. This suggests that children are naturally prone to appreciate and be kind when physical welfare is concerned. This makes sense because such needs are easily observable and universal. Another more advanced physical welfare theme—mentioned first by boys at age seven but then reliably by both genders by ages nine or ten—was *protecting a friend.*

Let's pause for a moment and see how we can put these findings to use. Adults can not only encourage these types of kindness, which are common for a wide range of ages, but they can also ask a child about any such incidences as a reminder to say thanks. The more a child learns to value these behaviors by saying thanks for them and doing them for peers, the more the child will have positive social interactions and opportunities to be grateful in the short run. Moreover, they'll improve their chances of closer friendships taking root, increasing opportunities for gratitude even more in the long run.

From Universal Needs to the Specific Needs of Peers

One interesting pattern we observed was the decline in descriptions of behaviors related to universal mundane needs and the rise in descriptions of behaviors reflecting more sensitivity to personal needs. Five- and six-year-olds mostly mentioned *cleaning up* and *returning things* as common helping activities. But by ages seven and eight, the kids mostly mentioned appreciating and doing more kind behaviors that were tailored to peers' individual needs or desires—such as *sharing personal items* (e.g., clothes, an umbrella, toys, jewelry, electronics), *helping learn something* (e.g., rules for a game or skills for a sport), and *helping with school assignments*. These are all behaviors that require greater sensitivity to specific personal needs.

Returning things to their owners and helping clean up after playing are appropriate experiences for five- to seven-year-old children. So using these teachable moments as they occur and emphasizing the golden rule—do to others as you'd have them do to you—help teach the importance of respect of others to this age group. Adults can easily encourage children to be empathetic by suggesting they share their snacks, for example, or by reminding them to help their siblings and friends when they get hurt at play. For seven- and eight-year-olds, however, beneficial social exchanges consist of meeting specific needs or wishes of their peers, which can be accomplished through sharing or by helping with school assignments. Thus, adults can ask kids of this age group about ways they could do this with friends or classmates. Needless to say, whatever your child's age, when he or she is on the receiving end of a kindness, a reminder from you to express gratitude by saying "thank you" always makes good sense.

Teach Your Child That Emotional Support Is Good to Share

Something special starts happening by the time a child turns eight. Our study found new themes emerging in the examples of kindness that students identified: *encouragement, emotional support,* and *social inclusion.* In general, students ages eight to ten began mentioning sensitivity to psychological needs as examples of appreciation and generosity. Examples of encouragement mentioned by boys and girls included cheering for friends and congratulating them on projects and in sports. Examples of emotional support mostly revolved around being there for friends who were sad, angry, hurt, or feeling ill.

We also found some gender differences. Girls provided more detailed descriptions of how they and their friend offered and received emotional support, citing such examples as hugging siblings or appreciating a friend's apology; and, by age ten, emotional support was at the top of their list of generous and appreciated actions. In contrast, for ten-year-old boys, social inclusion became a top generosity and appreciation theme; and the examples they mentioned mostly involved being included in larger groups (e.g., in play, games, sports, or school projects). For eight- to ten-year-old girls, social inclusion was not a top theme and examples revolved more around alleviating personal loneliness.

As a parent, you can encourage your children ages eight and up to give emotional support to their siblings and friends by making various suggestions, such as: helping a friend on a project, showing interest in something a friend cares about, inviting a friend to play a game or sport, or offering words of support during an activity or game they're playing. Adults can also ask kids if they have any friends experiencing trouble or any problems and identify what's wrong and brainstorm ways to support them. If you notice one of your child's friends is sad, worried, or angry about something, besides trying to help that child yourself, you can ask your child to try to help his friend himself. Kids of these ages should also be encouraged to thank peers who provide them with such gifts, too. Better yet, encourage them to say thanks and *also* do something kind in return.

Encouraging Empathy and Kindness toward Friends

Our study also compared how kindness themes for appreciation were similar to kindness themes for generosity. We found that each successive age group had progressively more overlap between the themes for appreciated behaviors and the themes for generous behaviors than the prior age group. This pattern of growth in overlap between generous themes and appreciation themes was clear: five-year-olds had around 26 percent overlap, six-year-olds jumped to about 43 percent, seven-year-olds had almost 50 percent, eight- and nine-year-olds were just over 60 percent, and ten-year-olds had 70 percent overlap. We interpreted the growing consonance between themes of generosity and themes of appreciation as an indication that more intentional generosity from benefactors brings about more genuine gratitude in beneficiaries.

Up to age eight kids' kindness toward others is mostly haphazard; young children tend to think everyone else enjoys the things they themselves like. Of course, what they like may not always correspond to what other kids would appreciate. Genuine gratitude doesn't develop until children, around age eight, are capable of putting more thought into how they can help others. Doing this requires them to consider peers' specific circumstances so they can better meet their personal needs. Though our data suggest kids become more in tune with other kids' needs as they approach age ten, adults should help and encourage younger children to be as thoughtful as possible when being kind. A little reminder goes a long way.

The above finding is consistent with what's known about the development of empathy—the ability to take other people's perspective and feel what they're feeling. Empathy leads to increasingly appropriate helping behavior. Encouraging a child to feel empathy toward another person will help her tailor the kindness offered. Many of the conversations between you and your child that we recommend in this book will help, but the more you teach a child to take the perspective of others (e.g., you, a sibling, friend, relative, etc.), the better and more in tune the child will be to another person's needs. This enables a child to provide more effective generosity to others, bringing more genuine gratitude to their beneficiaries, and ultimately stimulating closer friendships. Further, the more a child empathizes with her benefactors' efforts to be kind, the more that child can also experience genuine gratitude, which will strengthen those budding friendships. Fostering empathy, which helps your child be more generous toward others and more appreciative when others are generous toward them, will bolster your child's relationships and create reliable sources of gratitude.

Encouraging Thoughtful Thanks When Friends Are Kind

Recall the previous study on appreciation and generosity in children had students decide for themselves whether to provide examples of appreciation or examples of generosity. Across all age groups, children mentioned generous acts more often, about 60 percent to 80 percent of the time, than appreciated acts, about 20 percent to 40 percent of the time. This makes sense for a couple reasons. First, children often respond automatically to a friend's needs (as we discussed earlier, even toddlers do this), and, second, when kids receive help their joy or relief at first sometimes overwhelms their motive to thank.

No matter the reason, the fact that kids recalled generous acts more easily than appreciated acts suggests that it's especially important for adults to provide explicit guidance to young children when it comes to being thankful for kindness. Promoting positive attitudes about helping and encouraging kindness and thanking are excellent ways for adults to instill social skills in children and promote gratitude in them. The more kids understand and value generosity and appreciation, the more effectively they will use these behaviors in their social interactions, eventually making a habit of such thoughtful responding. Over time, such behaviors increase the chances that children will forge close friendships, which, in turn, opens them up to more opportunities to practice generosity and gratitude. As close friends help each other become more intentional helpers, they also help each other become more genuinely appreciative of their good fortunes.

So what's the take-home message? From the time kids are first able to speak, they are taught to be kind and say thank you to others to be polite. The first experiences with these behaviors in life are driven largely by politeness routines. What we're telling you, however, is that children can learn to be more thoughtful and deliberate with their "thank yous" and kind acts. Encouraging your child in these ways will help make the beneficial social exchanges in his life more genuine and meaningful. Greater understanding of moral behavior deepens trust and adds a level of satisfaction and meaning to our relationships, enriching our feelings of gratitude. Raising our children to develop moral maturity is one of the greatest gifts we can give our kids. So let's turn now to the strategies that help us support our children in acquiring and using their moral compass.

 **STRATEGY 19: Support moral reasoning in kids by emphasizing the effects of their behaviors on others, setting clear expectations for how to respect others, and explaining the reasons for behaving in these ways. Help them use moral emotions to make moral decisions for themselves.**

Children first learn the positive emotional skills they need to get along well with others from their parents and caregivers. Earlier we discussed how to promote empathy and to encourage caring in young children through sensitive responsiveness and authoritative parenting techniques. Strategy 19 offers additional and complementary techniques parents can use to provide their older children guidance that helps them build up positive emotional and behavioral skills through the adolescent years. The first technique is *inductive disciplining*, or pointing out the physical and emotional consequences of children's behavior on others, clarifying how they should behave, and helping them understand the reasons for these expectations. The second technique encourages kids to use moral emotions—empathy, sympathy, guilt, shame, and pride—to help them question and expand their moral reasoning and decide how to resolve moral dilemmas. We give special attention to empathy, as this emotion directly supports the capacity for generosity and gratitude.

Fostering Moral Reasoning and Behavior

Jenna had a good balance of responsibilities and worked hard to succeed. By most accounts, she was a good role model for others. When Jenna turned sixteen and started dating, her parents were happy to discover that she was quite discerning when it came to boys. She really wanted to date the kind of boy who was interested in her for more than just her looks. If she weren't convinced that a boy was sincerely interested in her as a person, she'd let him know that she just wanted to be friends. Though her parents trusted her judgment when it came to dating, they had one expectation that wasn't up for discussion: no sex until she was married. Jenna and her family were devout Catholics and pro-life activists. One day Jenna met Chris, a boy who shared many of her interests, and they got along perfectly. A strong sense of physical desire started growing between Jenna and Chris, but neither of them had adults they could talk freely with about these feelings and how to handle them.

Before meeting Jenna, Chris had unprotected sex a few times and nothing bad ever happened. Though Jenna was very reluctant to have sex, Chris convinced her that he was sterile and that there was no way he could ever get her pregnant. So there was nothing to worry about. They thought things like STDs or pregnancies happen to others, not them. Besides, they felt like adults. Several weeks later, Jenna discovered that she was pregnant.

Jenna now found herself facing difficult choices. What were they going to do? What was *she* going to do? Should they tell their parents? Of all the situations to be in, this was one her parents would never understand. She felt alone, confused, and angry. Jenna ultimately had to tell her parents, and, because of the family's religious beliefs, Jenna decided to carry the baby to term and find a loving family to adopt her.

Making poor decisions and failing to anticipate the consequences brought upon extreme stress, angst, shame, and a host of other negative emotions into the lives of Jenna and Chris. We have no way of knowing, of course, if in the heat of the moment anything could have altered the teens' decision, or whether their parents could have had greater influence on their children's decision making and behavior. What we *do* know, however, is that parents who teach kids how to reason through good and bad decisions foster moral reasoning, behavior, and emotions in their children. Such parents are using inductive discipline to develop their children's capacity to take the welfare of others into consideration and act accordingly as well as to feel good after good decisions and bad after bad ones.

It seems likely that both Jenna's and Chris's parents were using alternative parenting techniques—ones we don't recommend—either *love withdrawal* or *power assertion*, or both. Love withdrawal is the withholding of attention, affection, or approval from a child after he or she makes a mistake, which inhibits a child from learning to value unconditional regard for others. Chris's immature focus on his own needs alone in all likelihood stems from his parents' love withdrawal when he would disappoint them.

On the other hand, Jenna's parents probably used the power assertion technique with their daughter given their firm views about abstinence and abortion, leading Jenna to believe that she couldn't discuss physical romance with them. Rather than try to understand the kinds of romantic situations that Jenna struggled with, her parents weren't open to discussing her unique circumstances together, let alone suggesting alternative solutions that might have respected her needs as an autonomous person. Instead, they demanded that Jenna abide by their rules without question and may have responded to any deviation on Jenna's part with punishment, which is typical of power assertion. All too often, the end result of such parenting is a child who is confused about her life; fearful of or angry toward her parents; and, eventually, resentful of them. In Jenna's case, she ended up pregnant. Had she been able to talk honestly with her parents about sex and romance, she might have been armed with more knowledge and, consequently, made a better decision about how to handle having (or not having) sex with her boyfriend.

Love withdrawal and power assertion, unlike inductive discipline, do not support children's development of moral maturity. The behavior of Jenna and Chris was morally immature, and we're virtually certain that the lack of inductive discipline played a role. To illustrate our point, we'll focus our discussion on Chris's parents, though we could do the same for Jenna's parents.

Had they used inductive discipline techniques, Chris's parents would have established clear standards with which to evaluate his conduct, and whenever Chris made bad choices that had negative consequences, they would have had conversations with him to help him understand what to do differently in the future. During such conversations, they would have encouraged him to use moral emotions in thinking through dilemmas himself. For instance, say Chris promised his friend Keith that he would go to the movies with him, but soon after got invited to go to the movies with Mick, a more popular friend. Learning about this, his parents could have asked Chris to imagine how cancelling the earlier plan would make Keith feel (sympathy), how Chris would feel if that happened to him (empathy), and how he might feel if he went with Mick instead of Keith (regret). Had Chris's parents used inductive discipline with him, they would have explained to him what he should do when approaching a situation as serious as having sex. The techniques of love withdrawal and power assertion, which make a child emotionally insecure, are no substitutes for achieving the goals of inductive discipline: to reason and act morally.

There's no definitive research we know of that examines the role of inductive discipline in making grateful kids, but we have several reasons to believe that this parenting style will promote gratitude in youth. First, inductive discipline helps children master and internalize the moral emotions. This teaches kids how to balance respect of their own needs with the needs of others and develop a sense of right and wrong that treats everyone with equal consideration. Such understanding, known as *distributive justice*, is essential to forming character and the positive relationships that fuel gratitude development.

Second, developing character this way helps make kids more aware of the consequences of their actions so they understand how their choices benefit or harm others. As kids better see how they can benefit others, they'll be more able to see how others benefit them, and being mindful of the kindness of others is a crucial ingredient for gratitude. While there's no guarantee that inductive discipline would have made Chris more honest, sympathetic, and caring with Jenna, we can be certain that its absence played a damaging role in this life-changing event.

Encourage Empathy for Other People's Life Conditions

Up until now we've looked at the ways adults can promote gratitude in kids by supporting their prosocial behavior and moral reasoning. Beyond thinking and behaving morally, moral feelings also matter, and, as we've mentioned before, empathy is particularly important. As children become adolescents they begin thinking abstractly enough to empathize with groups, individuals, and other people's life conditions. Chris's actions indicate a lack of empathy for Jenna and her circumstances at home. His behavior makes us wonder whether his parents could have taught him to be more empathic toward others at an earlier age. This would have started by creating a more secure attachment with him early on and helping him to develop empathy, concern for others, and more mature social skills.

Parents should be alert to situations that call for empathy and share them with their children. This is very simple to do, and there will be many occasions when you can talk to your child about empathy. If your child comes home from school and tells you about a kid who was picked on, for example, you can model empathy and say, "She must have felt so sad and alone. Maybe you can talk with her tomorrow to see how she's doing." If your family watches any of the dozens of talent competitions where a contestant is teased or even ridiculed for his performance, you can seize the opportunity to talk with your child about how that person might feel. This may arouse sympathy or concern for the contestant or empathy if your child can relate to the contestant's feelings. Either way, encouraging moral emotions such as sympathy and empathy motivates concern and caring for others. Beyond teaching kids an emotional vocabulary, social interactions like these show them opportunities for kindness and empathy toward others and help instill stronger prosocial motivation in them.

The ability to feel good about prosocial choices and bad about selfish choices also strengthens prosocial motivation in children because such feelings support values for creating and sustaining positive social relationships. Another dimension of moral development involves adopting standards of right and wrong that serve as guides and deterrents for one's conduct. Self-control harnesses our willpower to focus our attention on higher standards and values so that we better resist temptation to act selfishly and, instead, behave morally toward others. Indeed, a person with moral character prioritizes moral values over other personal values and has strong convictions that he tries to act in accordance with by persisting and overcoming distractions and obstacles. Moral character is further strengthened if a child values the moral virtues of honesty, truthfulness, trustworthiness, care, compassion, thoughtfulness, and considerateness—all of which promote positive social functioning and, therefore, gratitude.

Building Self-Control

Self-control is "the capacity for altering one's own responses, especially to bring them into line with standards such as ideals, values, morals, and social expectations, and to support the pursuit of long-term goals." It helps individuals succeed in imposing their ultimate goals and plans onto reality, and it's associated with having better interpersonal relationships, better mental health, more effective coping skills, reduced aggression, and less susceptibility to drug and alcohol abuse and criminality. Self-control helps children learn to direct their attention and make the connection between being grateful for benefits they receive and think positively about their benefactors.

There are many ways to strengthen a child's self-control, some of which we've already discussed. For example, using authoritative parenting, encouraging children's interests, and helping them set and achieve their own self-selected goals have all been found to increase self-control in children. You can also play games with physical interaction such as Simon Says or Red Light/Green Light. Cutting back on activities that allow discovery of authentic interests, imposing goals on kids, or making kids sit for long periods of time only serve to reduce opportunities for children to practice their self-control.

Other practical ways to strengthen self-control in youth include teaching them to respond positively to correction or feedback and praising them when they use social skills that require self-control (e.g., listening, knowing when and how to interrupt, controlling their frustration, and reporting back after completing a task). Adults can also encourage kids to take on activities that build self-discipline, such as sports or music lessons, as well as promote personal responsibility, such as cleaning their room or feeding the dog.

Your good parenting skills and strategies can be undermined all too easily, though, by the biggest mixed blessing of life in the twenty-first century—the vast array of media, in form and content, available at will to our children. To protect the gains you've made with your child's gratitude, empathy, and self-control, you must also provide your child with guidance and structure for watching or listening to media. Many messages from the media not only discourage self-control skills and the virtues of respecting others and oneself, they promote just the opposite. You can, however, teach your children to be wise consumers of the messages they're bombarded with by the media and marketing.

 STRATEGY 20: Teach your children to be critical consumers of media. Place limits on screen time. Encourage kids to choose media with prosocial qualities.

Children and adults interpret experiences with media much differently; children cannot fully appreciate the commercial nature of media. Lack of real-world knowledge puts them at a disadvantage when it comes to evaluating the truthfulness of the media messages they're absorbing. As a result, whether we like it or not, media influences our children's development, especially their independence and their sense of right and wrong. This is especially true of children under the age of seven because their logical reasoning is still developing. If a child sees kids in a commercial laughing while playing with a toy, for example, she'll be more likely to believe that she'd be happy with that toy and want it as a result. She doesn't understand that the advertisement is intended to make the toy look like a prized possession. Therefore, when young children see an ad—and the average child sees 40,000 television commercials annually—they tend to believe what they see.

Limit TV and Electronic Devices

The level of TV viewing for the average kid in the United States is excessive and should be limited. On average, adolescents watch three to four hours of TV daily; by time they graduate from high school, they'll have spent more time in front of the TV than in class. Sure, there are age-appropriate shows on television that are both entertaining and educational, but moderation is a key virtue. Watching television is a passive activity, and, when unlimited, it's unhealthy because it distracts and demotivates children from the more meaningful pursuits of reading, family time, physical activity, and playing with friends—all things that make kids more grateful. The American Academy of Pediatrics states that excessive television also puts children at risk for unhealthy outcomes such as poor school grades and obesity.

Limiting your children's screen time is straightforward: tell them how much TV they can watch and mean it. How much TV watching is too much? Any amount that interferes with your child's social, emotional, and intellectual development is too much. In both the Froh and Bono households, screen time (which includes TV and video games) is limited to one hour daily, and maybe a little more on weekends or rainy days, usually as a treat. We understand that this can be hard for parents to enforce; letting your child watch TV while you clean up and prepare dinner makes life easier.

Problems will develop, however, when you lose track of time and realize that your kids have been watching TV for several hours each evening, every evening. We've gotten so wrapped up in writing this book that at times our children have gone *way* past their screen-time limits. But we've generally been good at consistently setting these limits for years now, so our kids love reading and seem to really know how to play independently with other children. Consistency is key.

Let's take a peek into Jeff's home. There's no background drone from the television. His daughter, Julianne, is having a princess tea party with Mickey, Baby, and Elmo, and his son, James, is using Legos to build a three-headed alien that spits lava. All of this imagination and creativity would be dormant if Jeff's children were parked in front of the television.

There are other things you can do to limit screen time. Ensure the TV is off during homework time and family dinners. Aside from minimizing the media's influence on your child's moral development, having no TV during these important times increases your child's odds of completing her schoolwork and gives you more opportunities to strengthen your bond with your child. With less consumption of electronic media, children will more often enjoy learning things in other, less commercial ways, and they'll enjoy socially interactive activities more. Factors that promote gratitude development in children—fulfilling responsibilities, enjoying learning, and improving skills in different domains—won't be weakened by the media's attractive commercial messages.

The American Academy of Pediatrics recommends that, as a

frontline tactic for limiting television time, parents do not put a television in their children's rooms. We mentioned earlier that the passive activity of watching TV or playing video games can be demotivating; for this reason, we've found it useful to have an explicit rule of *no* electronics before homework is completed. Giacomo and his wife found themselves repeatedly nagging Dario to do his homework when he was in first grade. After implementing this rule, Dario finished his homework with far less nagging. Such limit setting has other uses because it frees the child to become involved in meaningful activities, use his strengths and talents, become authentic, and build good friendships—qualities essential for genuine gratitude to take root.

Managing Content for Little Ones and Keeping it Positive

Parents should also make sure that children watch shows that are age appropriate and that meet their developmental needs. So *Team Umizoomi*, a show where the characters use math to help other small children with problems, is perfect for three-year-old Julianne; the fantasy action show *Transformers*, her six-year-old brother's favorite, is not. One time, James, made so aware by his parents of who can watch what show, screamed to his parents, "She's watching something that's inappropriate for her!" when Julianne walked in on a *Transformers* episode he was watching.

Beyond ensuring that programming is age-appropriate, it's also important to monitor the content of the media kids consume and encourage more prosocial programs and media activity. An American child who watches three hours of children's television programming a day will see 4,380 acts of altruism in a year but 15,330 acts of violence in that same time. Strong evidence from research indicates that abundant exposure to violent programming and video games is linked to aggressive attitudes, values, and behaviors. In a comprehensive review of more than a hundred studies involving over 130,000 male and female participants from around the world, researchers found that violent video games increase aggressive thoughts, angry feelings, physiological arousal (e.g., heart rate, blood pressure), and aggressive behavior, and that they decrease empathy for others and helping behavior. On the other hand, exposure to prosocial content is linked to altruism, positive interactions with others, and tolerance for others.

Thus, lots of exposure to violent content can make children more fearful of the world around them, less sensitive to the pain and suffering of other people, and increase the likelihood of their being hurtful to others rather than helpful—countering the self-control skills and positive social orientation needed for developing moral behavior and gratitude.

Media Influences on Adolescents

Media consumption poses more challenges as kids become teens. Boys and girls start questioning who they are and how they're different from others. As they try on different behaviors socially and struggle to fit in, they turn to electronic communications with peers to sort things out. With greater independence and confidence, teens spend less time with their families even though, as we saw in the last strategy, parental involvement is critical for helping teens build up self-control and learn to make good choices independently. Continuing to support their autonomy while maintaining and enforcing high standards gets tricky, but it's important to keep up if adults want to protect the investments outlined in this book and continue supporting the development of their child's gratitude.

Risk taking is normal for adolescents because they tend to seek out excitement and intense stimulation. They face difficult moral choices about the use of alcohol and substances, sexual activity, lying, cheating, and hurting others. Relationships with peers become more important, and some scholars suggest that media assumes the qualities of a "super peer" in the sense that teens imitate the behaviors of the individuals they see on TV and in the movies. As teens identify more with pop culture to establish their independence, this influences the kinds of friends and groups they'll join and the activities they'll do, even if bad for them. Therefore, having authenticity and supportive ties with peers and adults who care about them and their aspirations also protects teens from getting too caught up in ideals of being accepted by the "cool" crowd. In other words, teens' goals and personal development will anchor them so they're less likely to wholeheartedly identify with unproductive peers and role models and more likely to stay on the grateful path.

Know this: excessive media consumption has been linked to many public health threats, such as lack of physical activity, violence, sex, drug use, and alcohol abuse that compromises the health of adolescents now and in the future and impairs their prospects academically and professionally. We mention this not to scare you but to level with you about the influence media can have on kids' decision making and character. *Making Grateful Kids* offers a way to buffer kids from such pervasive cultural influences.

Can Gratitude Protect Kids from Risky Behavior?

If we haven't convinced you yet that gratitude can help protect children from risky pitfalls, allow us to share another finding from our longitudinal study about the acquisition of gratitude in adolescents. Teens who showed increases in gratitude during high school (Thrivers) not only had many assets for personal development, they also showed decreases in delinquent and antisocial behavior, unlike teens who showed decreases in gratitude (Deficients). Thrivers reported reductions in using alcohol and drugs, cheating on exams, skipping school, and being disciplined with detention and by school officials, and they also showed 10 percent less of these delinquency behaviors than Deficients. Further, Thrivers were less likely to tease, gossip about, hit, threaten, gang up on, or hurt peers.

Choose Friends Carefully

Even though you're reading this book and trying to make your child grateful, you know that your child will come in contact with kids who they may like but who aren't necessarily the best company for them and who may attempt to influence your child in potentially harmful ways. A teenager may envy the possessions of another—cool clothes, cars, electronics, the list is long—and while a little envy is okay, what's not okay is to let your child fall into the trap of judging friends by their things. While associating with popular kids may be fun because they're on the pulse of the latest trends, they may never be more than just fun. The more your child chooses her friends for their personal qualities rather than for their status and fun factor, the better chance she has of connecting to friends with good character and developing gratitude naturally through a more thriving social network.

In helping teens see the difference between friendships based on appealing qualities and shared interests, rather than on image and status, adults have no friend in the media. Marketing messages in the media encourage immediate gratification of pleasure and counteract moral reasoning skills and attitudes about generosity. Falling for these messages makes teens more susceptible to negative peer pressure as they seek to associate with peers who exemplify the qualities glorified in the media they consume. Relationships with such peers will be shallow, filled with conflict, and lacking in cooperation—not the kind of friendships we want if our goal is to make kids grateful. Help your children reject the "easy solutions" portrayed in the media and see through the shallowness of their pop idols by making sure you discuss the topics important to your teens. Use these discussions to guide your kids to mature solutions to the moral dilemmas they face so that your kids won't need to look to the media for alternative, dubious answers.

Teach Youth Media Literacy

As adults, we pretty much know that media messages are mostly lies; the "goods life" doesn't lead to the good life. But kids aren't so lucky. They have a much tougher time separating fact from fiction. Therefore, it's our job to teach them how to be critical consumers of media. If we don't, they could discount the value of exploring and developing their talents and surrounding themselves with people who support this growth in them, two reliable ways of being genuinely grateful in life.

As people who value youth, it's our duty to help kids be as authentic as possible to weather the storm of commercial messages and use media in smarter ways that will matter for achieving long-term goals and purpose in life. It's tough. But we must stay committed to the cause and fight the good fight, especially if our goal is to raise grateful kids. Failing to do so will create a generation of youth that grows up too fast and mimics adult behaviors too early—both of which will hinder their gratitude development dramatically. A major part of this effort is to teach our kids media literacy. There are many resources online for this, so we won't go into too much detail. But we can talk with kids as we watch TV together and help them deconstruct shows and commercials for what they are.

For example, if you're watching TV with your teenage son and a Jeep commercial comes on, ask him to tell you what he sees. It's likely he'll tell you that he sees a guy having tons of fun with male friends and, of course, beautiful women. Two questions, taken from the Center for Media Literacy's "Key Deconstruction Questions," come in handy here. You can ask your child, "What creative techniques does the commercial use to attract your attention?" Here you can discuss how all media messages are constructed with a creative language with its own rules, pointing out that in real life having a Jeep doesn't automatically get you girls. You can also ask your child "What values, lifestyles, and points of view are represented in, or omitted from, this message?" Here you can discuss how the commercial tries to convey that owning a Jeep will make you look "cool" while being outdoors but doesn't emphasize that many people enjoy the outdoors because it gives them a chance to connect to nature and with others—and most of these people don't own a Jeep!

Gratitude Makes Us Better to Others and Ourselves

Children and teens will experience the giving and receiving of kindness. The degree of thought they put into being kind to others, and how well they process positive social exchanges, will significantly affect their relationships and their opportunities to develop gratitude. The strategies outlined in this chapter help parents show children how to get the most out of these interactions so they can create new relationships, strengthen old ones, develop self-control and character, and become more grateful. This takes time, effort, and proper guidance from others. But from positive moral development comes the ability to understand rules, roles, and standards that help individuals, relationships, and institutions function smoothly. It's in this wider context of social cooperation that gratitude becomes particularly valuable to individuals and societies alike.

Every day, children and teens are faced with situations where they must make decisions to resist impulses for a healthier, happier life. Whether that's eating another cookie when their parents aren't looking, cheating on an exam, or gossiping about someone because they think it will make them fit in, their will is tested constantly. With guidance and self-discipline, they can learn how to respect themselves and others by resisting such temptations. We can also give our children the resources to be unmoved by media messages that encourage selfish behaviors so that contradictory external messages have less power over them.

By stacking the deck with the strategies of this chapter, we not only help children develop character and gratitude, but we also empower them to create a better world.

CHAPTER 6

Dealing with Consumerism, Media, and Materialism

*H*AVING NOT HEARD from his son in almost two hours, Sal's father was not yet aware of the wonderful moment that was about to unfold. Six-year-old Sal was clearly excited and proud, with eyes open wide as he ran up to his dad with an uncontainable amount of spirit. Out of a variety of materials, scraps, colors, shapes, and textures Sal had found in his room, he pieced together a dynamic picture of a mountain landscape with the sun setting. Sal was very keen to point out the tiny pool in the middle of this landscape and the four people, who resembled his family, swimming in it. Sal proceeded to thank his dad for the swimming lessons that summer. He was particularly happy about all the new places he would be able to enjoy with his new skill, and this was evident in the surprising amount of detail in the picture. Sal's artistic talent had truly reached a new level, and the spark in his eyes reflected it.

It's moments like this that let us know our children are thriving. Every child has a skill, talent, passion, or concern that produces a spark. All parents, teachers, and adults who care about children are familiar with these special moments. They're special because they help define children's goals, ignite their imaginations, and motivate them to improve themselves and do better by others. We're concerned that opportunities to experience such moments are under siege in our commercialized culture. Pervasive advertising and the fast pace of modern life in a youth-dominated digital era imperil our efforts to raise self-confident, morally centered, emotionally stable children.

In this chapter we show how gratitude can serve as a unique and powerful resource for protecting children from rampant materialism. We also lay out effective strategies for keeping kids' materialistic behaviors in check, steering them toward gratitude and, we hope, helping you kindle more sparks to light their talents and passions.

Media's Effect on Children

Marketing targets children's emotions, as it does with adults. Unlike adults, however, children under the age of eight don't really understand how advertisements affect their thinking. Actually, they may not even be able to tell the difference between a commercial and TV show, let alone realize that the advertisement is presenting information as fact, when it's not. Research suggests that children do not begin understanding the persuasive purpose of advertising until age eight. Children undergo rapid social, emotional, and intellectual development during early childhood. Their brains absorb everything in an effort to make sense of the world and master their environments. They're learning how to direct and regulate their attention, concentration, emotions, and behavior. Their desire to conform to their peers begins to accelerate by middle childhood and peaks during adolescence, the period when teens are trying hardest to establish an identity. All of these factors render children and, especially, teens vulnerable to the branding effects of marketing.

Kids can grow dependent on the passive stimulation provided by commercialism, blunting their natural capacities for the cognitively demanding and socially beneficial activities that are vital for healthy social development and for developing gratitude in particular. A child who's parked in front of the television or computer monitor for hours on end isn't learning how to be creative or focus long enough to solve a challenging problem; he isn't losing himself in a book or exploring his imagination through art; and he isn't learning how to be a good friend or develop physical skills while playing outdoors.

Jeff and his wife, Cara, noticed that limiting their children's TV time and filling it with alternative activities seemed to have produced great benefits for their kids, including greater emotional self-regulation, sustained focus, independence, and creativity. They put their realization to the test in a particularly courageous way—a sixteen-hour family road trip. At first, Jeff thought Cara and he were asking for punishment by confining themselves in an SUV with a fifteen-month-old, a four-year-old, and no DVD player. Instead, because Jeff and his wife have always encouraged "old school" play—drawing, finger painting, puzzles, Legos, Play-doh, catch—they were pleasantly surprised to find that their kids had developed the skills necessary to sustain a long car trip without digital entertainment. The kids thumbed through books, played peekaboo, gazed out the window, or listened to music and sang. Jeff's forced memorization of the entire soundtrack to *The Lion King* was the price he cheerfully paid for watching his kids grow, connect, and dream during this family vacation.

Children who sit in front of a screen all day are likely to fall victim to materialism. Such kids are seduced into a pursuit of commercial products and services that robs them of time for other experiences essential for their well-being and their capacity for gratitude. Having gratitude is a particularly effective way to ward off excessive materialism in youth because, as our research shows, the more grateful children are, the less materialistic they are, and the more materialistic children are, the less grateful they are.

Children become more materialistic when their self-esteem is threatened and they feel insecure. Adults who rely on "retail therapy" for a temporary and superficial bump in happiness when threatened with feelings of insecurity may recognize this association in their own behavior. Gratitude, however, boosts self-esteem because feeling grateful reminds us that someone cares enough to do something kind for us.

Learning appreciation and gratitude means becoming aware of one's strengths and interests and valuing oneself and others. Children become grateful by developing a reliable sense of belonging based on authentic friendship. By relying on possessing "the right stuff" to feel accepted and valuable, kids also unwittingly buy into a false understanding of true friendship and belonging, not to mention often impossible standards of physical appearance and accomplishment. Not only will this not make kids any happier, it could instill habits that in the long run suppress their self-esteem or capacity for gratitude.

Our next strategy helps reduce materialistic pursuits and encourage experiences and values that promote healthy social development and gratitude.

STRATEGY 21: Set reasonable limits on materialism. Offset commercial activity with experiential pursuits.

A Balancing Act

This strategy will help you reduce nascent materialistic habits in your child and counter them with behaviors that nurture independent thinking, authentic self-discovery, social responsibility, and positive social ties—all elements that are caused by and nurture gratitude. Materialistic behavior makes individuals and their sense of happiness dependent on acquiring things. The vulgar bumper sticker, "He who dies with the most toys wins," precisely captures this mind-set. This can lead to objectifying others and turning relationships into competitions.

Put materialism and gratitude in perspective by focusing your priorities on the quality of experiences in your daily life and your family's. Whenever your kids watch a TV program or movie, we suggest you have them do something before or after that requires them to use one of their skills, talents, or tap into their interests. Building on an interest piqued by a show is a great way to transition children into doing something noncommercial without their even knowing. After watching a *Little Einsteins'* episode about marine life, for example, an adult can help a preschooler learn more about whales by going to the library, getting a book on the topic, and reading it together. Similarly, a parent can help their child explore an atlas or a globe after a TV show that touched on travel and geography. For teens, an authentic activity to offset the commercial one might involve volunteering for a cause that concerns them (e.g., hunger, poverty, some illness, or the environment). Whenever possible, try to share in these experiences with them because these are interests and pursuits we can then continue to steer children toward to make them grateful. At moments like this, sparks of inspiration, passion, and creativity tend to fly.

Further, whenever a child or teen sits down to play a video game or electronic toy have them follow up with a visit to the park, another outdoor activity, or some reading time. Whenever your teen or your family as a whole spend time at the mall, try to offset it with an activity that involves giving rather than acquiring: help family members with a chore, assist a neighbor, or simply take a younger sibling for a walk.

Gratitude and materialism represent different ways of being in the world. To test this assertion and to develop our strategy of off-setting materialistic behaviors with experiential behaviors, we studied over one thousand public high-school students ages fourteen to nineteen. Our research showed that materialism and gratitude are opposing values that have consequences for adolescents' adjustment and well-being. *Materialistic teens* valued material possessions and considered them central to their identity and happiness. *Grateful teens*, on the other hand, valued people more, better recognized their blessings, and considered appreciation central to their identity and happiness.

Regardless of age, gender, and parental income and education, materialistic teens

* were less grateful toward others,
* had lower GPAs,
* were more envious of others,
* had less motivation to help others and improve their community, and
* were less satisfied with life (with their family, friendships, school, self, and circumstances).

Grateful teens, however,

* were less materialistic,
* had higher GPAs,
* were less envious of others,
* felt less depressed,
* were more engaged with activities that they personally enjoyed,
* had more motivation to help others and improve their community, and
* were more satisfied with life (with their family, friendships, school, self, and circumstances).

Reducing consumption habits leaves room for experiences (often free!) that our children can use to build more positive, supportive relationships. This strategy helps us be clear about priorities and how to organize around them. This need not be onerous; in fact, parents and kids might find themselves having a good time together by developing a list of activities they would enjoy doing. Such a go-to list will also help families stay committed to their plans to engage in such activities.

You may wonder whether adopting this rule would work with your children, who seem to be satisfied with the material possessions that their peers are touting. Perhaps you'll find the following research from the United Nations Children's Fund (UNICEF) convincing. UNICEF recently concluded a study that ranked the United Kingdom as having one of the lowest rates of child well-being among industrialized countries. A main reason cited for the poor ranking was lack of family time. UNICEF found that children in the United Kingdom actually preferred time with their parents to getting material goods, like toys and designer clothes. UNICEF also found that parents intuitively knew this, because they felt guilty for working long hours and tried compensating by showering their children with things. In Spain and Sweden, on the other hand, where family time has a greater priority, children were happier, even though they had fewer material items serving as parental surrogates. We believe the UNICEF findings confirm what we discussed earlier in the book: quality *and* quantity of time with our children matters, and they yearn for it more than we might think.

Limiting Material Consumption

Providing alternative healthy options to offset materialistic activity alone is insufficient. It's also necessary to limit your child's consumption of material goods. From age three and older, children begin to test limits as they seek independence. So parents, teachers, and other adults must make their expectations clear and give consistent consequences when children deviate from those standards. If a parent learns that his child impulsively blew every penny at the mall, for instance, the child should receive a consequence such as returning what she bought or losing her allowance for the upcoming week. Such limit setting can regulate children's habits of consumption. For example, parents may allow their kid to spend no more than 50 percent of their allowance on toys or clothes and require that the other 50 percent be put toward savings.

Setting limits on commercial pleasures has several virtues. It's difficult in today's world for children to avoid marketing because it's so pervasive. Keep in mind that it's not just products that are marketed to children, but a commercial lifestyle as well. As children come to want the products advertised to them, they also learn values, attitudes, and behaviors that encourage impulsive buying, self-indulgence, conformity, and mindless loyalty to brands. Such materialistic behaviors are antithetical to gratitude, and setting clear limits on commercial pleasures is important for making grateful kids because it teaches them the ability to delay gratification, self-discipline and self-control, and appreciation for what they already have.

Delayed gratification is sorely missing in today's media-driven youth culture, where just about any show, song, or game can be instantly accessed. As Peter Benson put it so eloquently in *Sparks: How Parents Can Ignite the Hidden Strengths of Teenagers*, teens "don't have time to wait, and they're surrounded by devices and environments that feed their impatience and restlessness. Teens' expectation of quick results and instant downloading has resulted in a lot of teenagers having a sense of entitlement." Learning to delay gratification serves to counter the sense of entitlement a culture of immediate rewards creates. Placing limits on a child's commercial indulgences helps parents reduce a child's nagging for the foods he sees on TV, that cool toy, or that violent video game he says everyone else is playing. Further, setting such limits establishes clear expectations of what a child can have, curbing the instances of nagging, and preventing a parent's guilt for saying "no" to such requests.

Grateful people know their strengths and priorities and appreciate those who help them in their life. We've found in our research that grateful children and teens don't believe that they deserve more than others and don't think that they deserve more things in life. They also don't assume they're owed respect or that they should always get their own way. Beyond quelling a sense of entitlement, though, offsetting commercial experiences and limiting consumer consumption provide structure and guidance to help kids manage their emotions and establish healthy habits for developing autonomy.

Perhaps the most powerful way to promote gratitude *and* counter materialism is to make a habit of giving to others, expressing thanks, and learning to savor gifts large and small. Our next strategy helps you and your kids develop such habits.

 STRATEGY 22: Give, thank, and savor regularly.

Giving and Thanking

Gift giving and expressing thanks are two basic, natural ways to become more grateful. So it's worth considering these behaviors again to see how adults can help young people do this. If you're like most people we know, you may not initially see the link between gratitude expression and decreasing materialism. But the answer lies in where we put our attention. When we express gratitude, our attention is focused on people who enrich our lives in ways we didn't expect. When we are engaged in materialistic pursuits, on the other hand, our attention is focused on ourselves and on things we don't have but wish we did. Our attention, whether it's focused on kindness from others or on material things, shapes our memories and attitudes about ourselves, those people, and even about the world. Social experiences involving gratitude fill our lives up with meaning and special relationships, whereas social experiences involving materialism fill our lives up with envy and shallow relationships.

Taking opportunities to be generous to others is not only one of the most reliable ways to give a quick boost to our mood, but it's also one of the easiest ways to influence how others see and treat us in return. As the most social species on the planet, humans are wired to reciprocate when it helps their survival. It means a great deal to friends or family members when you recognize that they could use some help and are kind enough to help them, especially when they weren't expecting your help. Your kindness then encourages them to reciprocate. Even small acts of kindness add up, and there is no better source of gratitude than to provide these socially supportive behaviors to one another. We've already discussed the importance of encouraging generosity for promoting gratitude in youth; now let's see how everyday thoughtfulness such as reciprocating favors and paying attention to others' needs can make a big difference in a child's development of gratitude.

College-bound Katie has a well-developed sense of gratitude, and it shows. At a high school graduation party Katie watches an old friend arrive. Being considered snobby by some, Danielle, pulls up in her BMW, wearing a Yale sweatshirt and clutching a trendy Coach bag. Rather than focusing on her friend's stuff, Katie actively listens to Danielle's updates about her life. She leans toward Danielle as she hears about her acceptance into Yale, smiles when Danielle mentions a scholarship, and asks questions such as, "What are the requirements to keep the scholarship?" Danielle, realizing the kindness implicit in her friend's sincere interest in what she has to say, reciprocates the active listening by responding enthusiastically when Katie tells her about her acceptance into Knox College and her loving relationship with her boyfriend. Positive reciprocity was ignited because Katie tapped into her gratitude for the friendship she shared with Danielle—and *not* her envy for Danielle's expensive stuff. Katie strengthened their relationship, in turn giving both girls something enduring to be grateful for.

Katie is old and wise enough to know how to focus her attention to strengthen her friendship, but younger children need explicit guidance. We suggest you help them see how they benefit from the goodness of others by using Katie's strategy. So while your child could leave a playdate feeling envious of his friend for having a Nintendo DS and all the latest games, you can help by refocusing your child's attention on how great it is that he has a friend who is kind enough to share. Such small nudges add up, and kids eventually do learn to value people over things, increasing the chances that they'll have more gratitude.

Savoring Your Good Fortune in a Culture of "Bigger and Better"

Another strategy to help increase gratitude and decrease materialism is to teach kids how to *savor*—the capacity to attend to, appreciate, and enhance positive experiences in one's life. Savoring is the ability to find the good within the good, and it helps counter *hedonic adaptation*. Hedonic adaptation is our ability to adapt to both good and bad events, as we discussed in chapter 1. A good event, such as winning the lottery or coming into a large inheritance, will only give us a momentary boost in happiness as we adjust to a new level of affluence and are back on the hedonic treadmill. On the other hand, a teen may think her boyfriend breaking up with her is the end of the world, a bad event, but over time she'll bounce back and have new knowledge that will improve her ability to face future breakups.

We tend to revert back to our emotional baseline. When our college students discuss hedonic adaptation, they often describe their experience with driving. They talk about how much better they thought their lives would be once they got their license and car. After a month or so, though, driving became just driving—a chore even. Had our students savored driving more, however, by exploring new places, visiting scenic destinations, or taking road trips to chat with friends or listen to music, they would have maintained a higher level of happiness longer, by stretching out the enjoyment of their car and stirring grateful feelings for their new gifts—whether the gifts be the car, the places, or the friends.

Savoring also keeps materialism at bay because the more good we find in what we already own, the more enjoyment we draw from those things and the less likely we'll feel the need to buy more. Let's face it: there will *always* be a newer, cooler, must-have something. Does it really make sense to be the kind of person who must be the first to get a hold of the latest smartphone or tablet, even though half of its fancy—and pricey—features will go unused? Sometimes "good" is "good enough." Does your current phone let you call people? Can you text a friend with it? Does it have Internet access? If so, then it sounds like you already have a lot to be grateful for— without the expense of a new phone or the hassle of having to learn how to use it.

We're not suggesting that you teach your kids to be cheap and pinch every penny. Instead, we're suggesting that you emphasize the value of three important resources: time, energy, and attention. Keeping up with the latest fashions and gizmos is hard work, and research suggests that being successful at this doesn't help us fulfill our basic human needs. Thus, to make kids more grateful and less materialistic, it makes sense to teach them how to savor what they already have so they can stretch their happiness and forestall adaptation.

Savoring need not be a solitary strategy; indeed, research suggests that sharing our joys with others is the best way to savor the past, present, and future. Reviewing old photo albums as a family, for example, is a phenomenal way to reminisce and savor the past, bring your family closer, and make your kids more grateful for their loved ones. Most of all, it meets a major challenge many parents face: providing their children with entertainment untainted by commercial messages.

 STRATEGY 23: Make opportunities for you and your child to share each other's worlds.

The Power of Old-School Play

Commercialized culture teaches children that nothing is enough as is. Clothing, toys, books, backpacks, shoes, and toothbrushes must have the brand of some beloved movie or TV show character emblazoned on them. Repeated exposure to such messages gradually encourages compulsive consumption, so that having one item or seeing one movie no longer is enough on its own. Taken too far, a child who watches *Sponge Bob: The Movie* in turn might not be satisfied unless he also has the backpack, toothpaste, yogurt, or whatever Sponge Bob accouterment catches his attention. Dr.

Susan Linn, director of the Campaign for a Commercial-Free Child-hood, suggests a child's immersion in products tied to TV shows or movies takes away the need to play creatively and saps the motivation to use imagination. The words children typically utter as a symptom of this unfortunate condition are, "I'm bored." Strategy 23 helps counter the automatic tendency adults have to simply give in to the consumer culture that awaits their families at every turn and encourages adults to instead find ways to have more time for imaginative and creative play with their children.

It's during such play that we learn about children's unique patterns of thinking and their inherent interests. Six-year-old Dario, Giacomo's son, gravitates toward animals and nature, a curiosity that first became evident when Giacomo played papa horse and Dario played baby horse, a game suggested by Dario. Baby horse would explore the plains and become tired or thirsty, and papa horse would find a safe place to sleep or a river from which to have a cool drink. Around the same time, Dario became the volunteer caretaker of chrysalises at his preschool. He'd monitor their development and look for signs of emerging butterflies, excitedly sharing his observations with his interested classmates and anybody else who would listen. Through the free flow of Dario's play and his caretaking role with the chrysalises, the adults in Dario's life were able to see an incipient interest in science.

Creative play helps us discover our children's intrinsic interests. It also demonstrates how being tuned into and reinforcing your child's interests, which we discussed as *sensitive responsiveness* in chapter 2, is critical during the creative play of a toddler or preschooler. Responding enthusiastically to children's ideas and creations shows appreciation and respect for the child's authenticity and independence. By taking or making opportunities to participate in the creative play children present us with, we have the privilege of peering into their universe, discovering their natural curiosities and strengths, and getting to know their unique character.

When too much of playtime involves commercial characters or themes, we lose these important opportunities. With commercialized play, children engage in superficial repetitions of scripts or scenes that never seem to stray far from the movie or show. Noncommercial play, however, provides opportunities to support our children's autonomy and frees them from the cheap fixes of commercial habits and unrealistic goals that inhibit their mind and spirit from flourishing. By encouraging originality and independence in children's play, adults can provide the language and experiences that enable gratitude. The more we do this, the more we help our children expand their creative and emotional repertoire and open their hearts to feeling the kindness of others.

Fulfilling Essential Human Needs

Recall our discussion of self-determination theory and the three fundamental human needs of autonomy, sense of belonging, and competency (as discussed in chapter 4). When valuing and achieving extrinsic goals such as wealth, image, and fame as central aspirations, people can become hindered in terms of fulfilling their fundamental needs, which can lead to feelings of emptiness and despair. On the other hand, when valuing and achieving intrinsic goals—such as kinship, friendship, and personal growth—as central aspirations, people can more easily fulfill the fundamental human need which supports mental health.

When you ask children with materialistic values what they want to do when they grow up, they either say they want to make money or they want to be famous. When you ask about their friends, they may describe the designer labels their friends wear or the cool gadgets they own, failing to appreciate or forgetting about the friend's personal qualities, achievements, or distinctive features. Ask a child with materialistic values if he believes he'll become a millionaire someday, and more than likely he'll say yes. Such responses show a lack of connection to a long-term perspective, aka reality. Most adults know that life requires a set of useful skills and abilities, such as being persistent, using creativity, networking with the right people, and seeking out opportunities for personal growth. In the long run, being actively involved in our child's world, we can better help our child accrue skills and resources that open up opportunities to grow, develop a positive identity, and fulfill her fundamental human needs by being actively involved in our child's world.

When Jeff worked as a school psychologist, he regularly met with Angela, a teenager who liked buying and owning stuff. She was obsessed with looking "the right way," and her mother—who was also preoccupied with looking good—encouraged this by hiring a personal trainer for her daughter. As time went on, Angela became severely depressed, eventually resorting to burning herself with cigarettes. We can't say that valuing materialism and behaving materialistically *caused* her problems, but it was clearly *related* with them. Ample evidence supports the theory that attaching too much importance on extrinsic goals can lead to fragile self-esteem, an inability to handle failure, major depression, and self-destructive behavior.

Once Angela's mental health was stabilized by psychotropic medication and psychotherapy, Jeff worked with her therapist to create a game plan. Employing strategy 23 Jeff made two suggestions:

1. Angela's parents should make spending time with her a priority, even if that meant saying no to some work projects.
2. The family should do something that they used to all enjoy doing together. When Angela was younger they liked going hiking in the woods. So he suggested they plan some hikes and appreciate Long Island's landscape.

While reluctant at first—the father called Jeff a hippie—they gave the suggestions a try. After only a few weeks, the girl and her parents reported their relationships got stronger. "It felt like the old days. I didn't realize how much I missed spending time with my parents and hiking. We're now planning a trip to climb Mt. Washington!" Angela told Jeff. So, with a little help from a school psychologist and caring parents willing to put first things first, the teen strengthened her relationships, developed new skills, and reignited healthy values—thus fulfilling her essential human needs and helping her thrive.

As the previous story shows, when families carve out opportunities to do things that fit with the personality, spirit, and character of each family member, they're authentically sharing each other's worlds. Such moments can be immediately gratifying and packed with things to appreciate, and they help kids focus on their natural interests while teaching them to appreciate the people involved in providing such positive experiences. In the long run, these moments help them accrue skills and resources that open up more opportunities to grow and develop a positive identity. The road to gratitude runs parallel to these things.

 STRATEGY 24: Counter complaints by encouraging children to appreciate the good in their lives.

Things Aren't So Bad

As we've discussed throughout this book, much of our happiness is determined by the social comparisons we make. When we compare ourselves to people we think are better off than us (*upward social comparisons*), we feel deprived; when we compare ourselves to people who are less fortunate than us (*downward social comparisons*), we feel grateful. A fundamental aspect of human judgment is that events, situations, and achievements, among other things, are not evaluated in isolation. Instead, they're evaluated in comparison to a reference point. Our happiness and gratitude are directly linked to the direction of that reference point.

For instance, a teen admitted to her second-choice college would feel upset, lacking, and maybe even envious if she compares herself to friends admitted to their top-choice colleges. Such upward social comparisons, if habitual, can lower satisfaction and hurt self-confidence. On the other hand, if she compares herself to friends admitted only to their "safety schools," she's more likely to feel appreciation, contentment, and a sense of abundance—and perhaps even develop some empathy toward her disappointed friends. In the long run, such downward social comparisons will help her learn that things don't always turn out the way we hope and that everybody has ups and downs; this knowledge will not only help dampen the sting of future disappointments but will strengthen her emotion regulation skills too.

Children and teens are good at focusing on how much better others—cousins, siblings, friends in the neighborhood, or friends at school—have it compared to them. From the time they are toddlers all the way up through high school, children are quick to focus on how others have more desirable possessions (like Legos or electronics) or circumstances (like pools or annual passes to amusement parks) than they do. Indeed, many continue to do this as adults. Such upward social comparisons produce dissatisfaction, and these feelings of *relative deprivation* can stifle an individual's ability to feel gratitude and appreciation.

Feelings of relative deprivation are falsely held beliefs that rest on cherry-picked comparisons, rather than the more careful observation that everybody has his or her own share of problems and discontents. Changing such a false belief, however, produces gratitude and appreciation by redirecting attention from what we don't have to what we do. In our own research, in fact, a consistent pattern always emerges: the more grateful kids are, the less envious of others and materialistic they also tend to be.

Things Can Always Be Worse

Recognizing that there are people who are less fortunate than us helps build empathy, gratitude, and appreciation. When we make downward comparisons with people who lack our comforts and necessities or who have serious problems or conditions, we put our materialistic wants in perspective and begin appreciating all that we *do* have. To maximize the effectiveness of making such comparisons, adults should help kids empathize with families they know who are struggling financially, suffering from serious illness, grieving over a lost loved one, or experiencing divorce. Discuss how difficult it would be for them to experience these things. Encouraging empathy like this will help kids appreciate their blessings, such as their family's financial security, health, or fortune for having two loving parents and an intact home.

Our research confirms what many other researchers are finding: materialistic people tend to be less empathic, helpful, and cooperative with others. They're so focused on their own needs that they fail to recognize that their relationships are usually short-term and characterized by conflict, competition, and envy. It should therefore come as no surprise that materialistic people are also less generous toward others and have trouble acknowledging other people's problems (e.g., poverty, illness, victimization, or discrimination). Recognizing that others may have it worse than us provides powerful teachable moments to promote empathy to our children and give them a new perspective on their materialism and what they often take for granted.

Generosity and Teachable Moments

Giacomo's friend Danielle has made a habit of using teachable moments with her five-year-old daughter. For instance, during a shopping trip to Target, they encountered a woman with her infant who asked Danielle for a small donation to help pay her rent. Instead of simply passing her by or giving her some loose coins and quickly moving on, Danielle came up with a great idea. She had a few bags of toys, clothes, and other necessities in her car that were bound for Goodwill. She told the woman they'd be right back and then told her daughter the plan. When Danielle and her daughter returned, they handed the bags to the woman. The woman was overjoyed with thanks and tears, and she praised them for their generosity. When they walked into the store, mother and daughter felt good about what they did, discussing how lucky they were that they had a home, a father, and a family; and when they walked out of the store they discussed how lucky they felt to have enough money to buy the basic things they picked up that day at Target.

The lesson was a lasting one. After that day, Danielle's daughter started a habit of looking for things the family no longer needed to give to poor families. There are always people or families nearby who suffer from hunger, chronic health conditions, and poverty. By helping people in need, kids get to see how they can make an impact on people's lives with little effort. These experiences foment gratitude by teaching children to appreciate the blessings in their lives and by showing children how life's better when people care for each other.

Holidays are ripe with such teachable moments and opportunities to acknowledge or be generous to others. Making a habit of such experiences with our children helps rekindle their appreciation for things that over time are taken for granted and boosts their contentment with how things are, leading to their developing more generosity and more gratitude.

CHAPTER 7

Nurturing Relationships

ONE DAY, Jeff's son, James, arrived home on the school bus looking a bit down and not at all like his normal zestful self. After a snack Jeff asked him, "Hey buddy, you seem a bit upset. What's up? Did something happen at school with one of your friends or something?"

"Not one of my friends, Dad. Jacob won't let me sit on the bus with my friend Ryan," James replied.

"What do you mean he won't let you?" Jeff asked.

"Every time I go to sit next to Ryan," James said, visibly upset, "Jacob jumps in the seat and tells me to sit someplace else, so I just do it."

Jeff and his wife, Cara, upset their son was being bullied, sat down with James and talked with him about how to handle the situation more assertively, including what to say to Jacob. The next day, James came bouncing out of the bus beaming. The plan worked; he sat next to Ryan.

Why did Jeff and Cara give this situation immediate and thoughtful consideration, aside from the obvious fact that they love James? For starters, James had had difficulties with Jacob before, and they didn't want his newly budding social life disrupted by hothead peers. Jacob was on the path to creating a toxic relationship with James. For a first-grader forming new peer groups, such experiences could leave an impression that social life is scary and deter James from approaching new potential friends at school.

Coaching Children to Navigate Their Social Worlds

Jeff and Cara wanted James to have tools to deal with this difficult social situation and quickly put the bad experience behind him. They wanted him to see social life as rewarding. James's emotional expressiveness helped them open the conversation. Left to fester, negative emotional experiences can prevent a child from engaging in schoolwork and from forming positive bonds at school. Your child's social development and friendships are fostered by his or her positive attitudes about and enjoyment of school. This is important to be aware of when your child is starting school, because social and behavioral competence predicts academic performance in first grade better than cognitive skills or family background. Therefore, another reason Jeff and Cara acted quickly was because they wanted James to engage freely in positive social interactions and relationships at school so he'd enjoy being there.

Relating effectively with others, as you'd expect, is critical for healthy social development. With friendships, children become their own person and gain a sense of self-worth. Initiating social interactions, maintaining social relations, and resolving interpersonal conflicts are valuable skills for developing social competence. This is why Jeff and Cara didn't take lightly to James's withdrawn reaction after encountering the school bus bully. They acted promptly to provide James with advice he could use when social conflicts erupt in his world. They told him to stare Jacob in the eyes and say, "You're not the boss of me; don't tell me what to do," and to simply maintain his stare and firmly repeat this statement if Jacob didn't listen. To make sure he'd succeed they also role-played this with him several times before he got on the bus again.

This story highlights the goal of this chapter, which is to help children grow positive interpersonal relationships with peers, family, and other adults and engage in and appreciate kind exchanges with them. Let's begin by considering the first steps parents can take to promote healthy social development and equip their young children with the basic skills for forming positive interpersonal relationships. The first caring relationships in a child's life have a long-lasting influence on how the child relates to others and his capacity for gratitude.

Opportunities to play and socially interact with other children at home or in preschool really matter. If you choose to nurture your child's social and academic development at home rather than send her to preschool, the next section includes some important qualities of preschools that can be advantageously replicated at home.

Choosing a Preschool

Parents can support their children's social development and early gratitude training by selecting the right preschool. Most preschools are privately run, and the National Association for the Education of Young Children accredits only 10 percent, so your own research and judgment will likely be your only guides to making the best choice for your child. Contrary to what you may assume, preschools that emphasize academic skill development by focusing on teacher-directed lessons and exercises to improve skills at the expense of play are probably *not* the best choice. Jeff and Cara knew they found a preschool that really valued play when they dropped in on one on a very cold and snowy day and saw teachers bringing snow into the classrooms with huge plastic bins so that the kids could play with the snow without the fear of frostbite.

Preschoolers need physical activities that let them use and coordinate all of their muscles, large and small. They need guidance from competent teachers and staff to learn about the world and about friendship and to develop social skills for cooperating and resolving conflicts with peers. All of this play will benefit children academically in the future. In particular, look for a preschool that provides the following features:

1. Daily outdoor playtime where children can run, jump, climb, shout, ride wheeled toys, etc.;
2. Classrooms filled with various toys and objects that they can creatively manipulate (e.g., painting, blocks, clay) and that have different spaces for reading, role playing, and moving around;
3. A blend of opportunities for children to work individually or together with others on different things; and
4. Teachers and staff who respond to children's individual needs, support their strengths and interests, encourage good decision making, and foster their emotional and prosocial development.

These are the features that matter. For instance, although his parents selected a great preschool for their son, four-year-old Max isn't crazy about the idea at first. Sensitive teachers will comfort him and guide him toward choosing an activity that interests him, just as they do with other students. Max discovers that he and classmate Kim like to play many of the same games. This gives rise to a friendship. Now that they're having fun, they start encouraging each other to interact and play with others. Thanks to a clubhouse and other props in the classroom, both children are playing house with several others they have invited to join them, each child taking on the role of a different family member. One child plays a baby crying for food, another is the older brother comforting her, and two others play the parents, with one feeding the baby and the other doing chores. When two children want to play the same role or with the same toy, a teacher steps in to help the kids learn to share or take turns.

The more children learn to play with each other and get to know each other better, the more cooperative play takes place. Such dramatic play in particular also supports the development of self-regulation skills because children learn to follow social rules even if they might not feel like it. Thus, environments with the features listed above create optimal conditions for self-control, social skills, and friendships to grow.

Social experiences at preschool provide a natural way for children to build their skills of reciprocity and cooperation, and, eventually, develop gratitude. This happened with Giacomo's son in preschool. Alex found a few friends he liked playing with and quickly warmed up and started engaging more and more with other students and teachers. He became close to one friend in particular, Zoe, so much so that one day several kids held a wedding for the two of them. The "newlyweds" soon started being emotionally supportive of each other. Alex would look forward to seeing her at school, and when Zoe was feeling down and missing her mother one day, Alex tried cheering her up by bringing his baby doll to share with her the next day. We can help kids build and nurture such healthy bonds with family members and friends by setting good examples.

 STRATEGY 25: Model positive relationship behaviors with family and friends by being generous and thanking others. Encourage children to do the same.

Modeling Generosity and Thanking

Consistent modeling is essential for teaching a child how to establish his own positive, healthy relationships, which make gratitude possible. It may take a while for children to pick it up, but, with patience and persistence, your efforts will pay off. Fred loves giving flowers as surprises and expressions of gratitude. After seeing this dozens of times, his son Billy, at age two, began picking dandelions and giving them to people. At six, Billy has graduated to giving his mom pink and red tulips for her birthday because, as he recently wrote in her birthday card, "I know you like pink and red." The point isn't that you must give flowers to say thanks; it's that if you want your child to have good relationships in his life, including the one with you, you must consistently demonstrate behaviors that will grow good relationships.

Creating a Culture of Appreciation

Of all the purposeful positive relationship behaviors that you could model for a child, there's one that we think trumps all others: making other people a priority. Many parents, ourselves included, at times fall prey to letting life dictate what we should and shouldn't be doing, rather than remaining in charge. In order to avoid sending mixed messages to your children about the important place they occupy in your life, create and maintain a system that enables you to keep your priorities in order. If you make a promise to your child, keep it. It's helpful to remember the big rocks and the little rocks we talked about at the beginning of this book. The big rocks come first, and everything else comes next.

Jeff's former principal, Andrew Greene, was a master at putting the big rocks first. Whether popping into a teacher's classroom for a brief observation and following up with a note that read, "Thank you for being such an amazing teacher," or getting to school early to make breakfast for his staff, Andrew always let Jeff and everyone else in the building know that they mattered. Jeff will always remember one occasion. While waiting to talk with Andrew one day, Jeff overheard him on a call trying to arrange a business meeting.

Andrew looked at his calendar and promptly replied, "Six o'clock. Nope, can't do it. My son has a basketball game, and I've committed to going."

Impressed, Jeff asked Andrew about his ability to put big rocks first, and his boss summed it up beautifully, "Our behaviors reflect our priorities, and it's important to me to show the people I care about that they're a priority."

Creating a culture of appreciation, one that makes others feel like they're a priority, is crucial for creating positive relationships that promote gratitude both within the family home and outside it as well. We create a culture of appreciation when we thank the people we care about sincerely, consistently, and in a timely manner so that they know that we recognize and appreciate their efforts; it also reinforces them for acting kindly toward us.

We also can model a culture of appreciation for children by extending such behavior to others outside the family. Like we mentioned before, early on children practice thankfulness as politeness, not genuine gratitude. Genuine gratitude begins when a child is old enough to understand and appreciate other people's motives for providing them with benefits. So when you help a friend, take a moment to explain to your children what the friend needed and why you wanted to help. By explaining what other people's needs are and how we're helping to meet those needs, we guide children's understanding of helpful social exchanges. This supports their ability to appreciate kindness and feel gratitude.

Encouraging Generosity and Positive Relationship Behaviors

Siblings and children close in age can spend more time together than with their parents, so relationships between siblings, cousins, and familiar friends provide great opportunities to practice behaviors associated with positive relationships and generosity. When it comes to helping kids form positive relationships—and giving them wellsprings for gratitude—it's important for adults to address both negative behaviors (conflicts and rivalry) *and* positive behaviors (cooperating and sharing). Let's deal with negative behaviors first.

Reducing Conflicts and Rivalry

Parents help set the right tone by limiting the comparisons they make between their children in order to minimize the sibling rivalry, or competitiveness, that inevitably ensues. Messages comparing kids against each other convey to them that they must compete with their siblings to win our affection.

You know the kind of messages we're talking about. During a dinner party with family and friends, all the children eat their dinner, except for your child, even though you served her favorite meal. You might snap, "Everybody else ate their dinner, why didn't you?" Or, after asking your kids to clean their rooms a dozen times, one finally does, but the other just keeps adding to the chaos. The sight of the messy room may be enough to make you erupt, "Your sister cleaned up her room, and instead you made more mess!" Comments like these fuel rivalries and encourage unhealthy behaviors that are at odds with gratitude. Children already use competition without help from us because their sense of competence is still maturing, so it's up to adults to help them channel competitiveness in more constructive ways.

While it sounds simple enough to avoid measuring one sibling against another, it's not. We use social comparisons all the time and often automatically to make sense of who we are and our environments. It takes real effort to restrain the urge to compare when it comes to our kids, but restrain we must. Messages comparing kids against each other convey to kids that they aren't equal in our eyes and need to win our affection, so we ultimately just make things worse.

Conflicts and rivalry are also common with kids because they're still learning to express their emotions, and they tend to overreact if somebody "invades" their stuff. Here's another scenario we've encountered: Ben catches his cousin Mason playing with his Nintendo DS and starts screaming bloody murder as he tackles Mason to get it back. The first parental move, obviously, should be to separate them and restore calm. Then it helps to step back and look at both sides of the conflict to mediate a resolution next, which is achieved by helping them understand each other's feelings and then express those feelings in a constructive manner.

For instance, maybe Mason took Ben's DS because he didn't have his charger and the batteries had ran out. Ben, who had gone to the bathroom midgame, was upset to find his DS taken from him and his game reset. Thus, the adult could help resolve the conflict quickly by helping the two understand each other's circumstances and have Mason apologize and promise to ask permission next time and have Ben loan Mason his charger. By helping kids empathize, understand emotions, and use words constructively to resolve conflicts, adults teach kids the social skills of getting along and being kind to each other—the same skills underlying gratitude.

If adults don't understand what kids are experiencing during a conflict and don't help them learn to communicate toward a resolution, this not only puts gratitude more out of reach but invites more severe problem behavior because we don't help kids address the causes of the conflict. Again, the keys to gratitude include giving kids unconditional love, nurturing their individuality, and teaching them about the emotions and social skills for acting constructively in relationships.

Encouraging Cooperation, Helping, and Sharing

Children practice generosity and establish healthy social ties by being more cooperative when they're playing with other children. In a classic 1932 observational study of preschool children, University of Minnesota sociologist Mildren Parten discovered that free play evolves into more mature cooperative play as children develop social skills. When children play cooperatively, they interact with others in a coordinated activity or game where there is a division of labor in service of a common goal. For instance, a group of children might decide to build an enchanted castle out of blocks of wood. One makes the moat, another makes the draw bridge, another erects fortress walls, and two others build up the middle of the castle. Cooperative play lets children interact with others on something of value to the whole group, express their thoughts and ideas, help others, and try out new things without worry of winning or losing. For these reasons, cooperative play promotes helping, sharing, negotiation, communication skills, social competence, and friendship formation—all ingredients for fostering gratitude.

Though most opportunities for cooperative play occur at school, parents should also look for opportunities to facilitate cooperative play at home. For instance, if a child has some friends or relatives over, and all the children are playing nicely—sharing, taking turns, or helping each other with something—adults should take notice and provide specific praise. Saying, "That's great you guys are playing so nicely," is okay, but giving some subtle guidance to your kids by mentioning specific positive behaviors (e.g., "That's great you guys are sharing your toys") is better. Children who aren't exposed to cooperative play or who don't make progress in learning to play cooperatively risk being excluded or rejected. Being helpful and cooperative, on the other hand, motivates children to reciprocate and be generous toward each other, increasing the possibilities for supportive relationships and friendships to take root. With such supportive ties in place, opportunities for feeling grateful and expressing thanks grow naturally in the context of children's social experiences.

Besides fueling healthy social relations and gratitude in the long run, generosity is motivated by gratitude, too. Along with University of Illinois marketing professor Lan Chaplin and colleagues, Jeff conducted a study in which two groups of teens were asked to keep journals for two weeks. The participants in one group kept a gratitude journal and those in the other group a daily journal with no reference to gratitude. The adolescents were given $10 for their participation at the end and told that while they were welcome to keep all of the money for themselves, they could also donate some or all of it to charity. This served as the measure of generosity. Teens who kept a gratitude journal donated 60 percent more of their money compared to those who kept a daily journal ($6.81 versus $4.23), establishing a strong link between gratitude and generosity.

Encourage Thanking

Until your children make a habit of expressing their gratitude, you should remind them to offer thanks so that such behavior becomes habitual. You should also teach your children to understand that there's more to expressing thanks than just being polite. Start by helping them include a brief mention of why they appreciated a gift when they write thank-you notes for birthday or other presents. It's also important to help a child be specific about the benefactor's personal qualities that made the gift special. So if a friend is always a good listener and knows exactly what your child would appreciate, encourage your child to mention this quality in their thanks. This will help your child provide more authentic and meaningful expressions of appreciation.

When kids are made to feel special and valued, thanking will come naturally to them. One summer, Mimmi invited her grandson, Giacomo's son Dario, to join her on a special train ride through the Rocky Mountains, which made Dario feel very grown-up. They got a sleeper roomette, read books, played games and puzzles, had meals, and talked about the many wonderful places they passed. Afterward, Dario's parents encouraged him to write a thank-you card mentioning the special things he enjoyed. His note included a long list of the sights he enjoyed most and a paragraph about how much he liked having the top bunk and using the miniature sink in the roomette. He also mentioned how much he appreciated her always wanting to do "cool new things" with him and knowing how to make him feel like a "big kid." As you can imagine, Mimmi's eyes lit up when she received it.

Forming Friendships

Through friendships, children gain independence and social skills. They learn cooperation, companionship, supportiveness, and emotional security. They also come to understand the importance of reciprocity and loyalty and acquire knowledge about social conventions. As they approach adolescence, they start gaining a sense of self-worth from friends. While listening to your child talk about his friends, be alert to any mention of him benefiting from one of these characteristics of friendship—and suggest he thank the friend who's responsible.

Some friends are better than others. Some elevate us and help us improve and flourish. High-quality relationships like these are one of life's greatest gifts, and good friends give us many reasons to be grateful. We turn to our closest friends to share our thoughts, vent our frustrations, and share exciting news. Oftentimes our friends inspire us to be better people.

While these benefits give us reason enough to value our friendships, we only feel grateful if we *recognize* them for the gifts that they are. So we must try to be mindful of this. It's easy, however, for us as adults to get lost in the busyness of life and be inattentive to the goodness of others, and it's just as easy for a child to take for granted the friend who texted them after a breakup, "Hang in there. It's their loss." So one thing we can do to help our kids develop and maintain healthy friendships is to teach them how to be mindful of their friend's kind acts, to savor them, and to express gratitude to them in turn.

 STRATEGY 26: Help kids be mindful of the unique benefits different relationships provide and to give thanks for them.

Mindfulness

Mindfulness, or our lack of it, has recently become a popular subject with psychologists and the popular media. Mindfulness keeps us aware of our actions and our environment in the here and now. Strange as it may sound, it's completely possible to act without mindfulness, thanks to a culture replete with information, stimulation, options, and distractions that can occupy or overwhelm us.

Because mindfulness makes us more attentive to the people with whom we are interacting, it helps us take interest not only in what the other person might be feeling or saying, but also more generally in their welfare.

When we're mindful, we monitor our thoughts and feelings and are less impulsive. If, for instance, your child is frustrated by her math homework and starts doodling, rather than lashing out at her and possibly saying something you'll regret, being mindful helps you remember not only that she has had difficulty with math before but also that today she dropped her favorite book in a puddle and therefore didn't feel like doing homework. Being mindful in this situation would prevent another battle over homework and help you understand your daughter's stress. This, in turn, could lead you to hug and reassure her that you're there to help, and maybe even compel you to bring out the blow-dryer to fix her book.

People who stay mindful during social interactions are more satisfied with their relationships and better at responding constructively when a relationship hits a rough patch. People who are generally mindful are better able to cope with stress and tend to experience less negative moods compared to their less mindful counterparts. As the example above shows, keeping our negative emotions in check makes us less likely to have negativity cloud our thoughts and dictate our actions. Further, mindful people are also better at communicating their thoughts and feelings to important others. When we're mindful around others, we're better able to give sustained attention to social interactions, which, in turn, helps us create and maintain rapport. Returning to the previous example, mindful adults will focus not on their own stress but on their child's, validating their child's emotional experience and helping the child feel secure in a time of vulnerability. As you can imagine, receiving such support is easy to appreciate.

Teach Children to Be Mindful When with Friends

Now that you have a better understanding of what mindfulness is and its role in positive, supportive relationships, how does it fit into making your child more grateful? Remember, in order for our children to be grateful they must first slow down enough to recognize all of the blessings in their lives. Being mindful does just this. Our society moves at lightning speed. We're in constant communication with others, whether it's about important or unimportant matters, and the majority of us are almost always somehow connected via technology.

Jeff recalls the last time he and his family went out for dinner. Sitting next to them were a family of four—two parents and two kids—all looking down, texting, and missing out on what could have been an opportunity to learn more about each other and strengthen their bonds. Think about it. How often do parents get a break from dinner duty and have the liberty to catch up with their kids on recent successes or struggles? Not often enough. But instead of seizing this moment, everyone in the family of texters missed out on a precious opportunity to connect and share. If this is common behavior for families—and we hear from a lot of kids that their parents are just as bad, if not worse, at controlling technology during dinner—should we be shocked that many of our kids are oftentimes mentally elsewhere?

Imagine a teenager on a class camping trip. Surrounded by nature, she has a great opportunity to bond with her peers. Instead, she's texting, listening to music with her headphones, and watching YouTube clips on her iPad—maybe even simultaneously. If she were to set aside these distractions, however, and focus on her surroundings and the activities therein, she could feel the live earth beneath her feet, embrace the sounds of birds singing, and relish the sun's warmth and natural wonders around her. This would maximize her experience, subsequently giving her opportunities to feel grateful. But, again, to do this she'd have to slow down and live in the present moment.

We're not luddites, and we're not suggesting you try to be. We're just using technology as an example of one of the many things that pull us away from the here and now. The point is this: if making a grateful kid is your goal, then everyone (adults and kids) must unplug and make room to reflect on the good in life. This allows us to not only savor the past and the present, but to anticipate future blessings as well.

Here's a scene we've encountered and bet that you have, too. Our child has a friend over, but fails to share his toys with his friend and pretty much ignores his friend's wishes. Needless to say, this is no way to help a friend feel special or even want to come over again, so it makes sense to encourage your child to ask about his friend's interests and suggest he pay attention to his friend's enjoyment while playing. In other words, coach your child to be mindful of his guests during playtime. This may even expose your child to fun in a way he hadn't considered before, helping him discover new interests—and all thanks to his friend.

Empathy Builds Gratitude

Being mindful helps make kids more grateful because it promotes empathy and helps them tune in to other people's needs and develop quality friendships. In one study, students were assigned either to a mindfulness-based stress reduction intervention or a control group that didn't receive the intervention. Those students who were taught how to be mindful were more empathic after their intervention was finished, and these positive benefits were still apparent three months later. This is important for gratitude development in kids because, as we learned before, the ability to put yourself in benefactors' shoes allows you to see their responsiveness to your needs and appreciate the value of their kindness.

Recall the school-based curriculum, discussed in chapter 5, that teaches kids to think gratefully and the three appraisals it trains in kids to help drive their gratitude—the personal value of a benefit received, a benefactor's intention to meet your needs, and the cost to a benefactor for helping. The degree to which we consider these specific thoughts determines how much we appreciate and are grateful for another person's kindness.

Let's assume Jenny struggles with science and her friend Arianna is a wiz. Let's also assume that Arianna loves softball, and she's a rising star, but she skips a softball practice to help Jenny study for their upcoming exam. Arianna's help bumped Jenny's quiz grade from a C to a B-. To help Jenny feel empathy toward Arianna for this kind act, a parent would emphasize how much Arianna loves softball, how good she is at it, and the significance of her skipping practice so that Jenny will understand what Arianna sacrificed to help Jenny succeed in science. When we do this with our own kids and the kids around us, the result is nothing short of magical: kids discover the value of a particular friend and consequently feel grateful.

We should appreciate that beyond supporting children's physical, emotional, and social needs as they grow, parents are also responsible for setting the stage for how kids view themselves, how they view others, and how they think others might view them. Indeed, it's our responsibility to teach them how loving relationships work, as these views are built in childhood and remain relatively stable throughout life. How we treat our partner, our children, and other people teaches our children how to respond to others. If we're good models, chances are that our kids will follow suit. This, in turn, will help set the stage for us to have a wonderful, positive relationship with them.

In today's world, the social media environment that surrounds us impedes our capacity to be mindful of the good qualities in friends, develop empathy, and figure out how to navigate social relationships with sincerity and respect. Our perceptions of ourselves and others are filtered through electronic interactions such as text messaging and Facebook, Twitter, Instagram, and other social media. Electronic communications such as these make it easy to simply be voyeuristic rather than genuinely connect with other people. We believe these social trends provide yet another reason why it's more important than ever to make grateful kids—because gratitude will help us maintain meaningful relationships, which is what makes us human.

 STRATEGY 27: Teach children to use the Internet, social media, and related technologies to maintain genuine connections with friends and family.

Adolescents are easily attracted to the stimulation of electronic media, which unfortunately makes them susceptible to negative influences and consequences. For this strategy, we focus specifically on how to use technology in prosocial ways to counter the objectification of relationships, whereby people try to improve their standing in life at the expense of others.

Any adult who cares about children knows that monitoring their use of the Internet and social media is essential to keeping them healthy and safe, both physically and psychologically. News stories and personal accounts abound about cyberbullying, which occurs when others deliberately and repeatedly use social media to torment a classmate or other child by sending messages or posting pictures to humiliate or denigrate him or her. Cyberbullies also spread rumors that damage friendships or ruin them completely. Helping youth learn how to use technology to enhance their relationships rather than hurt them is a challenge, but with the right guidance and support from adults, kids can use technology to strengthen their connections with people instead. Before we discuss concrete ways adults can do this, let's first briefly consider technology's role in creating and maintaining social relationships.

Technology's Effect on Peer and Family Relationships

Over the past fifteen years or so, technology has become increasingly important in the lives of youth, especially teens. Adolescents use all kinds of technology—instant messaging, e-mail, and text messaging—to communicate. They also use Internet sites for sharing photos and videos, social networking, and blogging. Contrary to popular belief, this technology is not weakening friendships among youth. Indeed, adolescents use these communication tools primarily to reinforce existing relationships, both with friends and romantic partners. Teens are also increasingly integrating these forms of communication into their "offline" worlds, such as using social networking sites to learn more about kids they might befriend.

Although electronic communication and technology may be strengthening peer friendships by letting teens interact when not in each other's presence, teens' relationships and communication with family members may be paying a price, with the parent-child relationship seeming to be the most affected. A four-year study of thirty families with children provides insight into technology's role in contemporary family life by capturing their daily interactions on video.

Here's what happened with participants in the study. When a parent walked through the door after working all day, her spouse and children were often so absorbed in what they were doing with their technological devices that they greeted that parent only about 33 percent of the time, usually with a quick "Hi." Even more alarming, about half the time the children ignored their parent altogether and continued interacting with their electronic gadgets. Upon receiving this cold welcome home, the parent often retreated to do something else other than spend time with her kids, presumably because she could see that her children were indifferent to her presence.

So while kids are using technology to keep in touch and connect with each other in new ways, their electronic multitasking has become so pervasive that it sometimes comes at the expense of face-to-face interactions with their siblings, parents, and even friends. This notion was supported by a study of 3,461 girls ages eight to twelve in which researchers found that tween girls' social skills and social well-being suffered because of too much multitasking and too little face-to-face communication. These researchers suspect that similar findings would hold with boys, but surprisingly, research is only now exploring this phenomenon. Thus, kids may be crowding out physical interactions from their social lives and consequently compromising the quality of their relationships suffering.

Consider how much we learn about ourselves and others and how rich emotional experiences are thanks to nonverbal behaviors like eye contact, gestures, touch, facial expressions, and other body language. Ignoring the presence of a parent, sibling, or friend isn't only rude, but it denies kids the rich dynamics face-to-face communication brings to social life. This may hinder personal development and the forming of strong social bonds. If being grateful and making kids grateful matter to you, then it's important to unplug and tune in to connect with people emotionally.

Help Kids Use Technology to Improve Relationships

The Internet is like a double-edged sword for schools just like it is for families. It has done wonders for education. With just a few clicks, kids can learn about the composition of sand, the origin of our universe, and the legacy of Dr. Martin Luther King Jr. While having easy access to such knowledge can improve learning, educators and school administrators are working tirelessly to meet the challenge of removing negative uses of technology while keeping its important advantages for learning. Families face similar challenges. So what can adults do to help youth use technologies to strengthen relationships? The multimedia nature of electronic and social media technologies have opened up an array of opportunities for expressing thanks and being kind to others in new and creative ways, and adults can be good models by e-mailing supportive messages to their kids during good or difficult times or texting a thank-you message to their kids when they raked the leaves without being asked.

When it comes to creative expressions of kindness, the roles are reversed and parents can count on their children's facility with such technologies. Kids already tend to share pictures, songs, or videos to lift friends up, motivate them, or make them laugh. They may forget to express thanks, though, so adults can encourage kids to send thank-you notes to friends or other people in their lives in the same creative ways. In addition, adults can remind them to follow up thank-you notes with an expression of thanks in person. Nothing beats the quality of live social interactions for deepening connections with others, and expressing thanks in person is a powerful way to experience gratitude, too.

Here's an example of how electronic technology can be used creatively in a prosocial way to strengthen relationships and promote gratitude in kids. Remember Dario's Star Wars birthday party, discussed in chapter 2? Dario's cousin Rosetta put together a special video for Dario's birthday gift. She gathered photos of Dario and crafted a gripping story of Jedi Dario battling galactic challenges to get to his birthday party. The video was complete with guest appearances from Yoda and various family members and the soundtrack of the main theme of Star Wars. It was so amusing that everyone at the birthday party watched it several times to laugh and discuss the plot turns. Dario's gratitude toward his cousin was clear: giddy from laughter still, he thanked her for such an "awesome gift." To this day the gift still warms the hearts of everyone in the Bono family.

Like strong family relationships, strong friendships are potent sources for making kids grateful because friends are people who love us unconditiotnally. We should help steer our children toward individuals who elevate them, not bring them down. This includes older peers, mentors, and adults outside the home. For the final strategy in this chapter, we turn to investing in such social relationships.

 ## STRATEGY 28: Help children build up social capital.

Though scholars in different fields have proposed various definitions of *social capital*, we use the term here to mean the supportive social ties outside the home that are critical to the physical health, moral development, and well-being of children and teens. Children acquire social capital by participating in social networks that benefit their immediate productivity (e.g., learning social or athletic skills or techniques for hobbies or personal interests) or their long-term success (e.g., learning skills that are advantageous educationally, professionally, civically). It's easy for parents, teachers, or neighbors to forget about helping youth to cultivate social capital. We each try to cope with daily challenges, often alone, and forget to consider the social ties that support youths' personal development. Families, however, can be proactive in cultivating and making use of social networks for securing quality information, advice, support, and protection for children; this can lead to positive outcomes for youth.

Help Youth Build Social Capital

Cultivating social capital is an important part of instilling gratitude in youth. It's how we make room in their lives for growth-inspiring experiences to occur; this is another important way that gratitude matures. Having social capital helps kids and teens explore their personal strengths and the issues they care about, and importantly, it enables them to determine their own path in life. Knowing how to step in and help a young person move forward—by giving your time, energy, and attention—are the greatest gifts adults and older peers can extend to children. When we lend a hand to a neighbor's kid struggling to put the head on top of a gigantic snowman, help another child with an ambitious project, or listen to a niece or nephew who may be having an issue with their boyfriend or girl-friend, we help those kids become more grateful. We discuss ways to help kids in our communities more toward the end of the book. But for now, let's consider how to grow the social capital of kids in our own care.

Scholars and philosophers have considered the importance of social capital for children in society. Much of this work, done by sociologists, examines how social capital helps children of lower socioeconomic backgrounds. Little is known about the actual role of social capital in child development, though.

"Virtue is never left to stand alone. He who has it will have neighbors." —Confucius

The truth is, relationships with peers and other people outside the family provide a distinct resource that parents cannot provide kids with as they develop into more autonomous beings. To illustrate, here's a story about a time when Giacomo and his wife, Kate, had dropped off seven-year-old Dario at karate one evening a bit late, and the other students had already started their stretches. Giacomo mentioned to the sensei that Dario had a bloody nose just before class, thanks to a collision with his little brother's head. Thinking that everybody heard this disclosure, Dario became embarrassed and reluctant to enter the dojo.

Giacomo and Kate tried to convince him that there was nothing to be embarrassed about.

"Anybody can bump their nose on accident," they said. That didn't work. "Nobody but sensei heard." That didn't work. So there they all stood in front of the classroom trying to resolve the matter calmly, with twenty or so kids trying to have class and Dario absolutely fixed on a detail his parents had no idea would get him so upset. As they were about to retreat to the car with hands up in the air, the sensei stepped in. He assured Dario that only he heard, mentioned that everybody in the class was waiting for him, and then asked the students to welcome him—which they heartily obliged. To his parents' relief, Dario kicked off his shoes, tied on his belt, and entered the dojo. Although Giacomo and Kate couldn't convince Dario to enter the class, they realized instantly that sometimes other people are best left to help.

When people take an interest in and help us we feel grateful. Jeff's experience with one of his recent undergraduates, Kyle, perfectly illustrates how helping youth develop life skills can make them feel grateful. One of Jeff's main goals as an educator is to help students relate their studies to their lives. Doing so not only helps them learn the material better, but it also helps them improve themselves. While some students have been kind enough to tell him that his course changed their life, the letter he received from Kyle reminded him why the classroom is his second home. Here's what Kyle wrote to Jeff after the semester ended.

> *Dr. Froh,*
>
> *Thank you for everything you have done for me. You have changed my life in a way that cannot be encompassed by words. I am in a much healthier state than I had been previously, and I really feel as though you have given me my life back. In my heart, I will always have an everlasting gratitude for what you have helped me accomplish in this short amount of time compressed into a single semester. Life is a challenge, and you have helped raise me back up to face it directly. There is so much that I could say, but the most effective way I can express it all can be done very simply. Thank you.*

As you can see, caring for others and being concerned about their welfare is a great way to instill gratitude. All Jeff did was what he does with all of his students; he got to know Kyle on a personal level, remembered his name and major, and taught him life skills such as how to nurture relationships, manage stress, self-motivate, and persevere. It was clear to Jeff on the first day of class that Kyle was bright, mature, responsible, and that he was a leader. Though he probably would've fared well over time because of such strengths, his letter to Jeff shows how far a little thoughtfulness and compassion from a community member can go for young people. So if you live in a community with kids and your goal is to help make kids more grateful, lend a hand and support them. You never know whose heart you'll touch.

CHAPTER 8

Developing Community, Connection, and a Sense of Purpose

*G*RATITUDE BONDS people together at the interpersonal level. As a human strength, gratitude helps people grow beyond themselves to forge stronger connections with family, school, community, society, nature, and God. To see how gratitude strengthens connections to entities beyond ourselves, let's listen to Barbara, a former student of Jeff's, describe her experience of reading a tribute in the form of a thank-you letter at her grandmother's funeral:

> *While I was speaking a breeze blew, and the petals from the tree behind me softly fell over all of the people listening. I knew this meant that my grandmother could hear me. I was crying, and when I finally looked up after the end of my letter I found the support of the entire gathering as they cried with me. Although my grandmother's gone, I still feel deeply connected to her and the rest of her family and friends who knew how special she was. I was so glad I did this even though it was terribly hard and uncomfortable. I didn't think this was possible, but I now feel closer to my grandmother than I ever have. And this feeling of closeness has made me want to reach out to her other grandchildren who are dealing with this great loss too.*

As this poignant moment demonstrates, experiencing *and* expressing gratitude connects us to others or to a larger purpose and motivates us to help and inspire others.

As a critical mass of scientific evidence showing the value of gratitude for children and adolescents accumulated and our impetus for writing this book grew, we started wondering whether gratitude might be unique in promoting optimal human development because of its wide-ranging benefits. According to positive youth development (PYD) theory, there are five Cs of PYD required for youth to thrive: competence, confidence, connection, character, and caring. Richard Lerner, eminent developmental psychologist, along with Peter Benson, founder of the Search Institute, helped develop PYD theory as a comprehensive approach to preventing risky behavior and optimizing youth development. Working with many other developmental scholars and youth development practitioners, Lerner and Benson found that having the five Cs produces the dynamics between youth and their real-world settings that best help them develop into thriving adults.

Lerner describes the five Cs in *The Good Teen*; *competence* is the ability to be effective in school, social situations, and work; *confidence* is an overall sense of efficacy and self-worth; *connection* is having positive bonds with people and social institutions; *character* is respect for societal and cultural rules and having a moral compass; and *caring* is having a sense of sympathy and empathy for others and a commitment to social justice. With these Cs in place, adolescents then develop a sixth C, *contribution*, which is a capacity to care for themselves and contribute to home, community, and civic life.

So far in this book, we've seen how supporting the first five Cs can help produce gratitude in kids. Let's build upon this picture and see how gratitude also has a special link to the sixth C, contribution.

We'll look at the importance of nurturing youths' aspirations and exposing them to meaningful causes that resonate with their values. We'll end by discussing how kids can use their creativity and unique intellectual skills to explore and find opportunities to contribute to greater causes in society.

Learning how to make positive contributions to society will give your children focus and motivation to discover greater meaning in their goals. Not only will this deepen and solidify their gratitude by giving them even more reasons to be grateful, but it will simultaneously start spreading gratitude to others, including institutions, eventually achieving a mutually reinforcing cycle.

Greatness through Gratitude

When we give workshops to parents and teachers on how to make grateful kids, we often raise the importance of teaching kids the *whys* and *hows* of being other-centered and finding ways to contribute to their school or neighborhood. Our research shows that gratitude has the power to ignite an upward spiral of community-centered service. In a longitudinal study we recently conducted with over seven hundred early adolescents, ages ten to fourteen, we found that teens who were more grateful reported a strong sense of connection to and passion for helping their community (i.e., social integration) six months later, compared to their less grateful counterparts. These grateful teens reported that statements such as "I love to volunteer" and "I would like to make the world a better place" described them perfectly. We also found that gratitude and social integration mutually enhanced each other. See figure 2.

We directly looked at gratitude's impact on teens' sense of purpose too in our four-year longitudinal study with over four hundred adolescents. We interviewed participants who ranked in the top 15

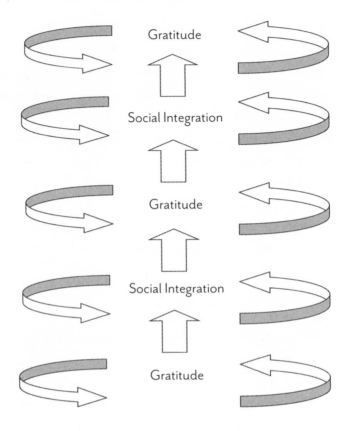

Figure 1. Gratitude and socal integration in an upward spiral of positivity.

percent of gratitude or the bottom 15 percent of gratitude at the beginning of the study about their sense of purpose in life four years later. The findings are intriguing. We'll discuss some of the main findings throughout this chapter, but we wanted to share one with you now that's relevant to our discussion of young people and social engagement.

Michael was classified in the top 15 percent of gratitude as a very grateful kid, and Brian was classified in the bottom 15 percent of gratitude as a very ungrateful kid. After discussing what they want to be different in the world or how they would describe their ideal world, both teens were asked "Are you doing anything about this?" Michael said, "I'm trying very hard to be as open-minded as possible when it comes to finding new ways to benefit the world." By contrast, here's what Brian said: "No. I feel like the things that I want for an ideal government take lots and lots of time to do anything about. So I don't think my ideal world could be achieved. I'm currently not doing anything about this."

As these responses suggest, gratitude may be the answer we're looking for to get kids to see and act on things beyond themselves and grow to be caring, contributing citizens. One of the first steps in this process is to interact with children in a way that allows us to learn their passions.

 STRATEGY 29: Be a good listener and a good interviewer to discover your child's passion. Help him identify a sense of purpose related to his passion.

"Why are you here?" When asked this question at the beginning of a new semester, many of our college students remain silent or perplexed. A few typically share the usual "I need the credits" or "Your class fits my schedule" or "I wanted to be with my friend." But we're looking for the deeper meaning behind the question. For example, we're both professors. Why? It's not because of the autonomy, flexible schedules, or summers "off." Though these are nice perks, they wouldn't have been enough to keep us committed to our education for so many years. There had to be something more that we hungered for: showing the next generation that we cared about them, that we believed in them and their dreams. We discovered that being educators and sparking serious dialogue on the importance of making grateful kids were great ways to achieve these goals.

It's this connecting to something larger—in our case, inspiring youth to greatness—that many youth lack today. The picture William Damon paints with his groundbreaking book *The Path to Purpose: Helping Our Children Find Their Calling in Life* provides a wake-up call. His research shows that almost 25 percent of U.S. youth ages 12 to 22 are "rudderless," have little to no direction in life, and are at serious risk of never fulfilling their potential. Another 25 percent have purposeful goals but have taken few if any steps toward those goals, and approximately 31 percent have actively tried several purposeful pursuits without knowing why they are doing so or whether they'll continue with these interests in the future. Only 20 percent have a clear vision of what they want to accomplish in life and why and have realistic plans.

We can help kids find their purpose by having open conversations, instead of adult-driven monologues with them, and, by being mindful as we listen, we can help them find the deeper reason for wanting to do something and develop a sense of purpose. Kids with a strong sense of purpose in their lives tend to be very grateful because they remain constantly amazed at what the world offers. They recognize the things they think are significant in their lives and are energized to share this insight with close others.

Damon and his research team found that having a sense of gratitude for being able to participate in something important in society and being able to make one's own contribution was a common theme among those teens considered to be high in purpose. For example, one of the highly purposeful adolescents said during an interview, "I'm starting to appreciate how special and wonderful it is just to *be*, and how lucky I am to be surrounded by people who exhibit so much love and beauty. I am so grateful and want to share this optimism and love for life with others. I guess that's how I find meaning." Gratitude tunes individuals into seeing the best in other people and in themselves. Importantly, gratitude helps teens harness their self-confidence and optimism and can inspire them to realize their highest ideals to, in turn, show the world what *they* have to offer.

Listen, Don't Lecture

Many conversations adults have with kids can be one-sided. Adults do the talking, and kids do the listening. This approach may be effective in mundane instances, like when you need to tell your teenagers how to best clean up the yard. But it's ineffective in instances where you're trying to inspire the best in them. In this latter instance, beyond being a good listener, you also must be a good interviewer and push them to gain insight into their own motives by frequently asking why they want to do something and why they want to pursue one experience over another.

You could, for example, ask your teenager to tell you about the things he really cares about or what's most important to him in his life and then find out *why* he cares about those things or *why* those things are really important to him. Further, when asking him about long-term goals also ask *why* those goals are important to him. Asking "why" is important because it helps kids become more aware of their inherent interests. As Damon reminds us, the parent's job is to "listen closely for the spark, then fan the flames." By asking the right "why" questions at the right times the parent can then provide teens with information to help them see the bigger picture and turn their interest into a more concentrated pursuit. This helps teens discover a sense of purpose, creating a wellspring for gratitude.

Rylee is a seventeen-year-old girl who loves animals, excels in biology, enjoys studying and learning, has great communication skills, and is very sympathetic and empathic. Without the proper support from adults it's possible that she might not consider that all of these qualities would make for an excellent veterinarian. But with some dialogue, some effective "why" questions from parents, and a little guidance and care from perhaps other adults, Rylee might discover this career option and be put on a path to purpose that she may have otherwise missed. Fast forward to her graduation as a doctor of veterinary medicine, and it wouldn't be hard to imagine the gratitude she'd feel toward her parents, teachers, mentors, and supporters who helped her form and reach this dream.

The activities youth gravitate to offer clues about where their path to purpose may lie. Attentive parenting will help you notice and reinforce instances of absorption in activities. Once you know what a kid is interested in, use this information as a springboard for two-way conversations between the two of you.

Sonja Lyubomirsky, the leading authority on happiness enhancement, says in her book, *The How of Happiness*, that if there's any "secret" to happiness it's in finding activities that fit you best. The same applies to civic engagement. If your adolescent loves playing piano and wants to join the band at school or orchestra at church, support her. If, however, she already dreads piano lessons, pushing her toward these things won't only make her dislike playing the piano, but it may also make her dislike band or church by association.

Just as you shouldn't dominate the conversation, your child shouldn't either. When a child shares interests and likes with you, you should keep in mind his strengths. Review the chart of strengths in chapter 2. This will give you a better sense of what your kid is good at, what activities would give him the best opportunities to use his strengths, and the experiences he would find gratifying and most appreciate.

For these two-way conversations to have a meaningful impact, they must occur regularly. We appreciate how time deprived everyone feels but, as we've emphasized before, it's critical to put big rocks first. That means ridding yourself of distractions and giving kids undivided attention for an extended period of time. It's easy for the hustle of life to pressure us into being quick with them or to squeeze out these important two-way conversations altogether. We, too, have fallen prey to this, but keep in mind that it's important to be efficient with things and effective with people, especially our kids.

Tell Kids What Gives You a Sense of Purpose

While it's critical to be a good listener during these two-way conversations, you should also share your life story as an example. Believe it or not, kids at any age love listening to stories of how we find purpose with our activities and our professions. Jeff and his family have dinner together almost every night of the week, and everyone recaps their day. This ranges from his three-year-old daughter, Julianne, proudly sharing how she finished her peanut butter and Nutella sandwich all by herself to his school psychologist wife sharing how she helped several students. During these conversations, Jeff's kids listen to Jeff and his wife share how their work gives them a sense of purpose and what they do to improve. These conversations seemed to have had an impact on Jeff's six-year-old son, James, as can be seen in this example.

JAMES: Dad, how old are your students?

JEFF: Eighteen and older, why buddy?

JAMES: Because I want to have students one day, too.

JEFF: That's cool. How old do you want your students to be? That will determine what level you teach at. Do you want them to be like your age? Olivia's age? Brittany's age? Mariah's age?

JAMES: I want them to be like Brittany's age.

JEFF: So you'd like to teach high school kids?

JAMES: Yeah.

JEFF: What do you think you'd like to teach?

JAMES: Division.

JEFF: That makes sense. You love math, and you're great at it. So maybe you'd like to be a high school math teacher when you get older.

JAMES: Yeah. That's what I want to do.

Whether James becomes a high school math teacher remains to be seen; three years ago he wanted to be a fisherman. The point is, conversations like this influence his thinking about what he might like to do in life. Had Jeff and his wife left their kids to wonder about their passions, a potential source of future purpose for James may have remained unidentified.

Not only do such experiences help adults bond with kids, they help kids find the things they care about, opening up opportunities to be grateful to people who support them in these areas. In Giacomo's home, discussions about how he and his wife, also a psychologist, study human behavior have helped their son Dario develop his interest in science. In his own way Dario has also assumed other values of his parents that will undoubtedly shape the formation of his purpose, such as caring for the environment. He's now learning all about the importance of protecting animal habitats and is sharing this passion with others—sometimes more than they would like.

Let's consider conversations and interactions Giacomo had with his father when he was growing up to illustrate how values and skills for forming purpose can be transferred to a young person. Giacomo would sometimes go to work with his dad, Rosario, who ran a ceramic tile installation and contracting business. Like most immigrants, Rosario worked hard, usually six days a week. If Giacomo asked if they could go home sooner, his dad would inevitably say that another step was needed to maintain the quality and durability of the job.

Rosario took great pride in his craft. The shortcuts other contractors used to finish jobs faster and cheaper were below his standards. Although the entire industry was moving toward cheaper ways of doing things, Rosario was steadfast in providing the quality of work he had learned in Italy.

Giacomo heard the admiration customers and friends had for his dad's craftsmanship. Bono Ceramic Tile was for discriminating customers, and he was successful thanks to word of mouth marketing. He saw the respect that contractors and vendors had for his father's craftsmanship. They lamented that Rosario was part of a dying breed. Such experiences with his dad provided a model of purpose and taught Giacomo the importance of using your strengths and talents to enrich people's lives through hard work and a commitment to high quality. Little did Giacomo know that this would nudge him to use his own strengths and talents to make a meaningful contribution to the world.

One way Giacomo's purpose was informed by his dad was by observing his dad be purposeful with his craft. The experiences with his dad also gave Giacomo "an initial moment of revelation" that something in the world could be corrected or improved. He learned that people rush to buy into quick fixes at their own peril. Some things, like your home, are too important to compromise because they are connected to our quality of life; it is worth investing in the quality and beauty of our home so we can better enjoy time with loved ones. Eventually, Giacomo would have a "second moment of revelation" that he himself could make a difference: he realized the value of gratitude in a world where people so often labored for more and more things that in the end mattered little to their well-being. These three factors—observing people being purposeful, noticing there are things in society to be fixed, and realizing that you can help fix those things—are processes involved in purpose formation.

Much of the quest for purpose falls outside the home. Once you have a better sense of what really excites your child, you can help him find opportunities in your community that resonate with him. This brings us to our next strategy; helping children become active members of society.

 STRATEGY 30: Help kids become active members of society. Increase their civic engagement.

Unfortunately, today's youth are less likely than earlier generations to demonstrate key qualities of good citizenship such as attending religious services at least monthly, reading newspapers at least once a week, working on a community project, attending club meetings, and believing that people are trustworthy. Civic engagement is a barometer of the future of democracy. Therefore, those of us who live or work with youth should make nurturing civic-minded kids a priority.

As kids become aware of political institutions, larger communities, and social issues, they become active citizens by volunteering, belonging to groups, consuming news media, and discussing issues. These actions will shape interests and pathways for them to develop a sense of purpose. During late adolescence and young adulthood, individuals' path to purpose is better defined and driven by personal values. This motivates them to create the kind of world they envision for themselves and for future generations.

But for youth to develop a true sense of purpose that connects them to something larger than themselves, they need help from the adults in their lives to provide opportunities for them to become more civically engaged starting in childhood. When doing this, it's important for the activities to be age appropriate (e.g., you could trust a twelve-year old to sell hot chocolate at a local Christmas tree farm, but it might be unsafe to let them cut down the trees). Further, if a kid enjoys the activities, they're likely to be engaged throughout, thus increasing the chances that they'll participate in the future (e.g., a child might enjoy making sandwiches for the poor, but an adolescent may instead enjoy helping to build a house with Habitat for Humanity). There are no hard-and-fast rules here. Use your judgment. Let kids themselves have an active role in choosing how they want to improve their community. The more they're onboard, the better the experience will be for them (and you), and the more likely they'll want to help again.

How Much Help?

When trying to make children civically engaged, you must consider what level of participation or commitment is reasonable given their age, maturity, and other obligations. Being civically engaged includes participating in organized clubs; volunteering at a hospital as a candy striper; tutoring other students who are struggling academically; or visiting the elderly at a local nursing home. But it need not be limited to such worthy endeavors. You can raise a civically minded child beginning as young as age three, if you broaden your definition of what it means to be civically engaged.

Let's say you bring your child to the public library to borrow one or two books for the week. Point out the small acts of citizenship in this context, such as being quiet while getting the books to respect others who are reading or working and returning the books on time without damaging them so other people can read them. You'll be teaching your child how to be other-centered, a value essential to civic engagement.

Now think of an overscheduled, overworked teen who's lost a friend to drunk driving and learns that his new school has a club that helps students present education and prevention messages about underage drinking and other harmful acts to their peers through school and community activities (e.g., Students Against Destructive Decisions [SADD]). You could brainstorm ways to trim his obligations in order to join this club and be an active member. This may open up opportunities to be involved in the community in yet other ways.

These examples both suggest that the specific circumstances of a particular youth—age, strengths, areas of personal interest—must all be taken into account to help him or her be more civically engaged. Further, as the second example shows, learning about social issues that matter (e.g., bullying, drunk driving, drug use), especially for teenagers, is also important for motivating civic activity.

Modeling Civic Engagement for Kids

A theme throughout this book is the idea that modeling behavior for your children is important. They can pick up our bad habits just as they can pick up our good habits. It should be no surprise that civically engaged parents are more likely to have civically engaged kids. The behaviors we're talking about here could be something as small as keeping your community clean by always throwing your garbage in the trash, silencing your cell phone during a religious service to respect others' wish to pray and participate, or turning off the water at a camp when you're done so more resources are available for others. Though none of these examples are grand acts of citizenship, per se, the message they send kids is that being concerned for others' welfare and acting accordingly is a virtue worth cultivating because everybody benefits.

One day, while his neighbors were on vacation, Jeff heard a loud crash outside. A huge limb from his neighbor's tree had snapped off and hit the ground. Jeff decided to break up the debris, tie it up, and place it by the curb so his neighbors didn't have to return to such a mess. Sometime later, Jeff and then-two-and-a-half-year-old Julianne were sitting on their porch waiting for Mom to come home from work when a piece of newspaper blew across their lawn and landed on their neighbor's lawn. Julianne ran over, grabbed the paper, looked at Jeff and said, "This on Hans' lawn. I put it in da garbage." Julianne demonstrated that she knew caring for each other and their community is important by imitating her father's behavior.

The civic behaviors you model for your kids can be mundane, such as helping a neighbor with house maintenance. They can also be more involved. For example, say you're active in your church and teach religious education to kids, serve candy at the annual summer festival, and help out with other special events. Seeing this, your kids now want to be involved. So your ten-year-old son helps with the church's fall and spring cleanups, and your teenage daughter is an usher at the service. As these examples show, modeling any behaviors we want our kids to adopt plays a central role in making our kids who they ultimately become. If making your kid more grateful is one of your goals, which it probably is because you're reading this book, helping them become more other-focused is a must.

After helping youth identify what they'd like to do to make a difference in other people's lives, the next step is to support and nurture kids in their civic pursuit. We all bring different gifts to the table. In strategy 31 we focus on helping teens tap into their creative and intellectual resources to promote civic engagement and find a sense of purpose.

STRATEGY 31: Encourage youth to use their unique blend of intellectual skills, interests, and strengths in practical and creative ways that could benefit society.

Most readers would agree that the formation of purpose doesn't always come easily or quickly. As preeminent child psychologist Erik Erikson noted, adolescence is a period of exploration, reflection, and experimentation; and the challenge of establishing a positive identity and direction in life takes time to resolve. This may be very difficult in today's world. More information is available than ever in history, making youth feel bewildered by the options. Also, more young adults are working part-time because fewer full-time positions are available to them. These endless options coupled with limited employment opportunities available to young adults make it even tougher for parents or others to help young adults sort out how they might use their strengths and talents to reach their highest goals in life and commit to productive adult responsibilities

Help Young People Find Their Own Passionate Path in Life

Jeff approaches his work with zest and a sense of purpose because he teaches his students the skills for living a meaningful, fulfilling life. He wouldn't be teaching today, writing this book, or possessing the caring teaching style he does today if it weren't for the small teaching college he attended and one very special professor who took interest in him, William Thieben.

Before Professor Thieben reached his hand out to Jeff—figuratively and literally—Jeff had only read one book, *Boyz 'N the Hood*, cover to cover of his own will; every other book he'd read was a school requirement. But after many conversations with Professor Thieben, in the school café or on a dock overlooking the Great South Bay in

New York, Jeff discovered a passion for reading. His interactions with Professor Thieben transformed him because he realized how critical it was to have caring mentors who take a personal interest in you and who model positive behaviors, such as reading and supporting others. He also saw the importance of being a lifelong learner and the privilege it was to be a teacher. Though Jeff's been fortunate to have had many wonderful, supportive professors over the years, he's convinced that if it weren't for Professor Thieben living by the adage "to teach is to touch a soul," he might never have found one of the things that bring him a great sense of purpose: teaching.

The previous example shows how the right people in the right community can set us on a path to purpose. The same was evident in Giacomo's life. Besides the modeling of purpose and revelatory experiences Giacomo had with his dad, his parents also supported him in getting the skills and experiences he needed to pursue his passion to write and make a difference in society. Like many patriarchs in immigrant families, his dad just wanted Giacomo to find a career that made money, but his mom made sure that they as parents supported him in his dreams too. Let's see how he had to be creative in his path.

In college, Giacomo took interest to literature and writing. A dedicated English teacher helped him develop his own writing style. She introduced him to poetry readings, and then they self-published a book of the poems they compiled. During that time, Giacomo became intrigued by literature that showed the power of supportive relationships to transform people. He instantly took to this topic because as a child he caught encephalitis and ended up beating the prognosis of life in a wheelchair thanks to the prayers of loved ones who believed he would pull through. In graduate school, he gravitated to the topic of forgiveness and youth programs because of a few devoted professors. In Michael McCullough's Evolution and Human Behavior Laboratory at the University of Miami, Giacomo discovered the study of gratitude.

Eventually, Giacomo met Jeff and the two of them embarked on a journey with fellow psychologist and University of California, Davis, faculty member Robert Emmons that lead to a research grant from the John Templeton Foundation and to this book. Fortunately for Giacomo, both of these achievements came just months before his dad passed away. But this was the winding road that Giacomo took in finding his purpose.

Gratitude's Forward Motion

As the examples show, other adults provided invaluable help to Giacomo and Jeff finding their own ways of contributing to a greater cause. The beauty of this mentoring system is that it passes along gifts from one generation to the next, making gratitude central not just for individual well-being but for inching society forward. Here's a special example of how the gift Jeff received from Professor Thieben was passed on to Laura, a former student who e-mailed Jeff to say thanks. Here's the e-mail she wrote to him:

> *Hi Dr. Froh!*
>
> *I hope all is well with you and your family. I just wanted to take a minute to thank you. Because of you and your class I completely changed what I was planning on doing with the rest of my life, and I could not be happier. When I took your class I was going to get my Master of Fine Arts (MFA) here and hopefully become a poetry teacher. But I didn't. In the beginning of the semester you told us that we should love what we do. That was probably the best advice*

*anyone has ever given me! I didn't love what I was doing.
I was really good in poetry. I was teaching the intro class
here at Hofstra, and I had been published a bunch. But it
wasn't where my heart was. My heart was in special education and kids with disabilities transitioning from high
school to the workforce or college.*

*Your class and all the readings really made me eval-
uate a lot. I was graduating that May and was already
accepted to the MFA program. But in February I with-
drew from that program and applied to the rehabilitation
counseling program here at Hofstra—where my heart was.
The program had everything I wanted, and I could pick
a focus (youth transitioning) and also counsel those with
disabilities. Before your class, I don't think I applied to
this program because I wasn't comfortable enough with
myself. It sounds so silly to say. I was a 21-year-old and
wasn't confident enough in myself to help others with disabilities because I fully didn't accept myself. You did that
for me. So your words—do what you love!—had a huge
impact on me.*

*I'm now doing what I love. I'm in my second year of
graduate school here, graduating in December 2013, and
I couldn't be happier. I'm now interning, and last semester I worked with the young adults transitioning into the
workforce. It was a 4-month intensive program, and there
were 37 students. They all had disabilities, mainly behavioral and learning disabilities. It was challenging, and I
loved every minute of it! Each one of those students came
to hold such a special place in my heart because they all
have potential. They just didn't see it. They recently graduated from the program. And I was asked to be the guest*

speaker! I now have a select group of students that I'm in the process of finding jobs for. I actually just placed one the other day!

Thank you for pushing me to follow my dream, to follow my heart, and to use what I'm good at to help others. You really changed my life.

As this story beautifully illustrates, encouraging young people to do what sparks their passion and resonates with them and to use their strengths and talents is an ideal way to make them more grateful because it connects them to a larger cause and helps them forge a sense of positive purpose, which then is passed down and helps everyone feel like they're making a difference.

Something you'll appreciate knowing about Laura, if you haven't guessed already from her heartfelt thank-you note, is that she's one of the most grateful students Jeff's ever had the pleasure of teaching. Other strengths that make her unique include courage, love, kindness and generosity, and social intelligence. But what you may not have guessed is that Laura herself is physically disabled and confined to a wheelchair; she can't walk, can barely move her arms, and her neck is essentially fixed. Yet she lights up every room she enters. Her smile is radiant, and her laughter infectious. With all the conversations Jeff had with her, he *never* heard her complain. Quite the opposite, she was always focused on "how can I make today better than yesterday."

Courage and Perseverance Help Kids Find Causes That Matter

When you compare Laura to Brian, the adolescent in the bottom 15 percent of gratitude in our longitudinal study, you see stark contrasts in their attitudes and approach to life. Laura has clear, self-selected long-term goals that connect to meaningful causes. Brian doesn't. When asked about his long-term goals Brian said, "I want to maintain my workout routine," a self-focused goal that had no mention of helping others. Further, it's clear that Laura is committed to achieving her goals. We can't see much stopping her perseverance. With Brian, however, it seems like a change in the wind could alter his plans. When we asked if it was hard to stay committed to his academic goals, Brian replied, "It's been hard to remain dedicated to school. I worked hard but I didn't enjoy it. It was hard to stay focused on certain things." As Laura's story illustrates, it sometimes takes courage to explore causes you care about and persistence in using one's intellectual abilities and unique skills and strengths in practical ways before the path to purpose becomes clear. Further, when you compare Laura to Brian a clear picture emerges: youth with a sense of purpose are also very grateful.

Today, creativity and an entrepreneurial spirit are essential, and trends indicate that young adults have healthy amounts—even in the face of a recession. It's worth considering one other part of Laura's story. Like many other young adults, she started finding purpose working with an issue that personally affected her once she was ready to commit to that cause. We have come across countless stories of teens being grateful for making a similar discovery; they're grateful to be able to make a difference to others in an area that they struggled with personally.

But even Laura needed to get creative before she found her purpose. She was going to just continue doing what she was good at, poetry, without sufficiently exploring her options. In fact, research shows that creativity and using one's intelligence outside of academics (i.e., in a practical way that leads to a career path) both become important sources of self-esteem for older teens. Laura became empowered once she discovered a field that allowed her to use her unique skills creatively to make an important impact on other people.

Developing a sense of purpose could be hard without a personal issue readily available in a young person's life, though. When that's the case, creativity matters even more; youth must search harder to learn as much as they can about the issues they care about to get practical. This is consistent with evidence from a 4-H study of positive youth development conducted by Richard Lerner's lab. In this study of youth in grades eight through ten, those who consumed news media communicated more with parents about political issues, which predicted more civic duty, social connection to their neighborhood, civic efficacy, and civic participation.

To follow their dreams, teens must push themselves to search, be patient, commit, connect, learn, network, gain the right experiences, find role models and inspiring adults, and they must trust that doing this will pay off. Gratitude helps teens build the trust that they'll connect to something bigger at the end of the winding road— the ultimate quest in life. Again, our longitudinal data shows that those teens in the thriving gratitude group have more role models and caring adults at school as well as more extracurricular activities, as compared to those in the deficient gratitude group. Further, though teens in the thriving gratitude group attended religious service no more than teens in the deficient gratitude group, the thrivers reported being much more spiritual, which helps give meaning to their lives and draws them to transcend themselves.

All adolescents must truly explore and go through some amount of crisis if they're to find the issues they care about and a career path that resonates with them. They then must commit to the steps needed to succeed in those areas. This is how a mature identity is achieved. They cannot accomplish this alone though.

 STRATEGY 32: Create supportive environments where youth and their highest aspirations are valued and nurtured.

Before we dive into strategy 32, let's start with a thought experiment:

> *Think about your own sense of purpose in life. What is it? Is it to raise healthy, kind kids? Is it to increase the presence of youth and families in community events? Is it to develop a deep, meaningful relationship with God and to do God's work? Your answers to such questions will vary because they rest on your unique life story. So take the time to really identify what gives you your greatest sense of purpose. In other words, think about what makes you leap out of bed, stare life in the face, and say, "I'm doing this!"*

> *After pinpointing the burning motivation inside you, the next question we want you to consider is this: What factors have helped you develop this sense of purpose in your life? Okay. Now put down the book, get comfortable, close your eyes, and start reflecting. We'll be here when you're done.*

While the first question is interesting to us, and we'd love to hear what drives you every day, we're more interested in the second question. If you're like the thousands of parents and teachers we've worked with, your response was probably something along the lines

of having the support of one or a few caring people and being surrounded by others who valued you and your dreams, even if they
themselves didn't share the same vision.

The final strategy for this chapter discusses what parents and
other adults can do to help youth get the social support they need
to make a difference in the world, achieve their aspirations, and not
only develop a deeper level of gratitude but become a source of gratitude to others.

Show Youth That You Care about Them and Their Grand Ideas

If we want our homes and schools to be institutions that help kids
get a sense of purpose, institutions that value them as people and
their dreams, we need people like Professor Thieben. We need people who are active listeners when speaking with kids and mindful
during the conversation, not distracted by what they want to say
next; we need people who accept kids' aspirations nonjudgmentally,
even if the aspirations aren't what they think is worthy of pursuing;
and most of all, we need people who care.

William Sefick, Jeff's friend and former colleague at a school district where he worked, exemplifies these traits perfectly. Bill was
a school psychologist for over thirty years at the high school level.
Being a "kid person," he always did more than was expected for the
students. Helping super high-achieving students cope with their
demanding schedules and workloads was one of his main missions.
The principal never asked him to do this, probably because these
kids were below the radar due to their lack of behavior problems.
Indeed, they're usually the ideal student. But they walk the halls
feeling the pressure of the world on their backs. Bill knew that
someone had to support our next politicians, doctors, CEOs, and

teachers; given his skillset and role within the school, he was in a perfect position to do this.

So week by week, month by month, year by year, Bill would counsel the valedictorians and other super bright students on how to cope with high stress levels, anxieties, and depression. With Bill's continued support and nurturing, many students went from experiencing life as an exposed nerve ending to calm self-possession. So dedicated to supporting young people that even in retirement Bill still communicates with former students while they attend college, helping them achieve their dreams and find a sense of purpose. And there's no shortage of thank-you cards from students that come Bill's way. We need more people like Bill in our kids' lives to support them on their journey. All it takes is one caring adult to make a difference. Be that adult.

Be Open and Nonjudgmental

As we briefly mentioned before, one of the best ways to create a supportive environment for kids is to be open to their ideas, flexible in what you think constitutes a worthy pursuit, and nonjudgmental of their dreams. When a young person trusts you enough to share her aspirations with you, your response is critical to keeping and strengthening your relationship. Even if the idea seems ridiculous, or just not something you'd want her to pursue, listen. And deep down she'll really want you to go a step further by sharing in her joy.

Consider the following scenario. A teenager wants to be an artist and is willing to work minimum wage and live in his car until he makes it big, unlike thousands of others. His parents want to support him, but they keep pushing for that boring Plan B (i.e., getting a "real" job unrelated to his passion). What should parents do in this situation? Should they let the school of hard knocks teach their teen that freezing in a car overnight is overrated? Should they demand that he follow Plan B for a steady income and benefits? If you want to show teens that you value their dreams and want them to succeed, we suggest something in the middle. For example, while they're painting canvasses on the side as a hobby, maybe even selling and displaying some occasionally, they could work in an art gallery. Perhaps they could start as someone who keeps the place clean, then move up to a salesperson, then to an assistant manager, then to the manager, maybe ultimately opening their own gallery someday.

We understand that the outcome for the teen in the above example is picture perfect (pun intended) and it assumes many things (e.g., he could find a job in an art gallery, the gallery had positions available at each rung of the work ladder, the teen was able to get a loan and space for his own gallery, etc.). Our message, though, is straightforward: when supporting a young person's pursuit of purpose, be nonjudgmental of the pursuit and be as supportive as possible, even if it causes you a little grief and a few sleepless nights. Adolescents tend to have intense feelings and ideals. That "nobody understands them" is a common worry. Take it from us. We've heard from many young adults of how important it is that people "get them" or "get where they're coming from." Not only do they say they appreciate adults' support without judgment, the gratitude is evident in their faces.

Another thing parents need to consider is that they should be flexible with what they think should give their kid a sense of purpose. Remember, what gives a sense of purpose to one person may not do it for another. So if a seventeen-year-old comes to you and wants to raise money to save a local bird that's at risk for becoming extinct, help her brainstorm how she can do this. Don't shoot down her idea because you think helping to purify local drinking water is more important or achievable. Being nonjudgmental and supportive won't only increase the chances that she'll be successful in getting a sense of purpose, but it will also show her that you think she matters and pursuing her goals is worthwhile.

There are, of course, times when adults *shouldn't* support young people in their pursuit of finding a sense of purpose: when their choices could hurt them or others. If a teenager's dream is to become a runway model and you learn that she's doing unhealthy things to her body to look the part, it's your job to step in and do everything possible to redirect her toward pursuits that will help, not hurt, her personal growth and development.

Cut the Cord

Beyond showing kids that we care and being nonjudgmental of their dreams, another way we can create supportive environments that show kids we value them and their aspirations is to do something that may seem counterintuitive: let go. Support and guide kids only to the degree needed for them to be successful. Anything more is too much. You want your children to have ownership of their pursuit and the outcome, successful or not. If they're successful, that's wonderful and something to be grateful for. If they're not, while unfortunate, help them use it as an opportunity to learn.

To illustrate, let's say a high school senior wants to go to college. Helping him develop a list of schools is excellent support, but researching the schools yourself is overkill if your goal is for him to own this task. Further, it's okay to review his personal statements; it shows that you care about him and his goals. Writing any part of it yourself is a complete no-no, assuming you want to support more than his attempt to attend college. If you want to support his autonomy development, confidence enhancement, and transition to young adulthood—you must let go. Letting the teen take ownership of the college application will give him the courage and motivation needed to pursue his dreams. He'll be grateful knowing that he'll always have your support—though from a distance.

Parents Need Help, Too

Helping youth develop a sense of purpose so that they'll become grateful might seem like an intimidating and overwhelming task, especially when you, like many, may have struggled with identifying your own sense of purpose. You can increase your confidence in helping a kid find purpose if you appreciate that the results of your efforts will take time, maybe even considerable time. A parent's influence has an impact on her kid in the long run, and a parent may not even fully see the mark she's left on her kid's life until after their kid has left home. It's therefore important for parents to realize that they shouldn't try to create a specific sense of purpose for their child.

Trying to identify what exactly will bring their kid purpose is, William Damon maintains, similar to parents thinking they can choose their child's personality or write their life narrative. What parents and adults can do, however, is introduce options, help kids find inspiration, and help connect them to people who can empower them down that path. Parents should encourage youth to find additional role models and discuss ways they might do that, if necessary.

By following the strategies in this chapter, parents and adults are more likely to expose youth to options that resonate with their own values and that will, as they get older, help them fill a valuable niche in the world they'll soon be responsible for building. This will make them more grateful because not only will they come to recognize and appreciate the many people—parents, neighbors, teachers, mentors, coaches—who helped them carve out their own unique path, but they'll appreciate that they have been given an opportunity to express their authenticity while connecting to a larger cause. The ultimate function gratitude may serve in human development then is helping youth find their own life story for elevating others in important ways and making a difference in the world. Gratitude may just be the best gift you could pass on to kids.

Chapter 9

How the World Could Be with *Generation G*

*A*LL CHILDREN have some skill, talent, or passion that produces a spark. It's the responsibility of parents, teachers, and adults to fan those sparks by feeding their children's curiosity and helping them create a positive and coherent life story. That journey begins when the child is born. When parents tune into an infant's needs and curiosities and satisfy the infant patiently with love, they're planting the seeds for gratitude to grow, even though there's no story yet. With love and more love, gratitude will help create the story. While this love is being given, adults must continue supporting their child's independence and teach their child about emotions and how people think. Eventually, the child's unique set of strengths and talents will emerge, and gratitude will sprout. When that happens, children become connected to a social world that cares about them and believes in them.

Gratitude is born of loving connection and grows from loving connection. So as adults encourage children to tackle challenges and learn from the consequences, whether they succeed or not, and as adults encourage children to grow and improve from these experiences, other people who care about them will take note and invest in them to fuel that growth. The more grateful a child is for such blessings, the more the child will soar and help others do the same. This was evident in the Westmont College women's basketball victorious season discussed in chapter 3; gratitude not only inspired the players to pull their coach out of her grief, but it pushed them all to surpass their own expectations of themselves. Gratitude like this helps people come together to achieve more than they could ever imagine and to understand that such feats don't happen alone.

The power of gratitude, though, lies in the passing on of these blessings. The mounting challenges of the world require us to figure out how to work effectively together because there are no magic solutions. Children must learn to work with the conventions of society and bring some innovation, no matter how small or large, to make life better for others and for themselves. This is how their strengths, skills, and interests come together to fill a valuable niche in the world. In chapter 8, we saw this in Laura's courage to follow her heart and use her social skills and particular strengths to help other kids with disabilities succeed at transitioning from high school to work or college. The ultimate function that gratitude may serve in human development, then, is to help individuals find their own life story for elevating others and to make a difference in the world. Like the *moral memory* of humankind, gratitude reflects the story of the best that individuals, and society, can be.

The Message of Making Grateful Kids

Before reading this book, you knew that raising grateful youth was a worthy goal. The specific steps needed to reach that goal, however, may have been a mystery. You now have the necessary resources to meet your goal successfully with thirty-two concrete, scientifically based strategies for making grateful kids. While each strategy is important in isolation, there are ten essential themes that underlie the strategies. These are guiding principles that will help you implement the individual strategies.

THEME 1: MAKE RAISING A GRATEFUL CHILD A PRIORITY

Of all the themes, this is the most important. Indeed, failing to make raising a grateful child a priority will lead your child to be as grateful as he was before you read this book. We're all pulled in a million directions, and it's easy to lose sight of what matters in the daily hustle. But you can do something about that. The solution? Put first things first. There's no quick fix for cultivating gratitude in young people. There's no gratitude pill. But be patient. Change will happen. The longer you remain committed to using the strategies in this book—and you may have to do this for the duration of raising your child—the more rewards you'll reap. Anything worthwhile takes a lot of time and effort.

THEME 2: MODEL AND TEACH GRATITUDE

Our children want to be like us. That's a fact. We provide the blueprint for what to say and what to do and in what contexts. One of the major ways kids learn this is by watching us. You should therefore get into the habit of adopting the specific linguistic style of grateful people. They tend to use words like *gifts, givers, blessings, blessed, fortune, fortunate, lucky,* and *abundance* when talking about their lives. Further, beyond learning to talk gratefully, you can show your thanks even more by developing your writing skills. We strongly encourage you to read *Gratitude Works* by Robert Emmons for ways to refine your thank-you letter writing. Make a habit out of sending thank-you cards and notes to friends. Help them in return if they've helped you.

Expressing gratitude through words, writing, and small gifts or acts of reciprocity are all ways to teach children how to become grateful. Doing this will help make your appreciation for the goodness in your life more public, showing your kids that blessings abound and that being thankful is a valued attitude. If your kids witness any of these simple yet beautiful acts, perfect; if they don't, tell them. A little tutoring goes a long way in fostering their gratitude development. And remember, little eyes are watching you.

Little ears are listening, too, and to temper a child's attention, some training helps. Remember, adults can promote gratitude directly in children by helping them appraise the benefits they receive from others. You do this by helping them appreciate (1) the personal value of benefits received, (2) the altruistic intention of people providing the benefits, and (3) the cost to those people. This helps kids think gratefully. Encouraging kids to consider these three appraisals when expressing thanks to others is also a powerful way to experience gratitude.

THEME 3: SPEND TIME WITH YOUR KIDS

Another way to spell love is T-I-M-E. Believe it or not, children and, yes, even adolescents, like being with their parents. One of the greatest gifts you can give your kids, a gift that will give them much to be grateful for, is your time. Quality of time matters, but the quantity matters too, so get into the habit of frequently sharing each other's worlds. Giving a child a lot of quality time with you teaches them the language of love—life's greatest gift.

Savor every moment together, big and small. This will give you and your child a heightened sense of appreciation for the things both of you love and for your relationship. While interacting with your child, act as if it's the first time that you're together. This is a creative way of considering your child's interests and choices in a new light and a fun way to be mindful around them and get to know them better. Remain curious about your child's fears, dreams, and everything in between. Getting to know your child can take a lifetime. Start now. And enjoy!

THEME 4: BE MINDFUL WHEN WITH YOUR CHILD

Many people think that quality of time spent with kids is defined as doing something their child likes, or something that's active, such as playing in a park, rather than passive, such as watching TV. But we take it a step further. While taking your child to a park is a great way to bond, it's crucial that you're completely present, physically *and* mentally. That means ridding yourself of all distractions at such times, including your smartphone. Be with them, fully absorbed in the moment. When you start drifting, and that's normal, return to the here and now and center yourself by taking a breath. You'll immediately be transported back to the present.

Being mindful helps you maintain empathy toward a child, and this provides important modeling of empathy, the most important emotion for developing gratitude and moral behavior. Being mindful *and* empathic toward a child allows you to discover a child's strengths, skillsets, and concerns and helps you be more supportive of a child's growth. Beyond strengthening your bond with children, all of this will help them become grounded, caring individuals.

THEME 5: SUPPORT YOUR CHILD'S AUTONOMY

Very early on children try to develop a sense of autonomy. Parents play an essential role in promoting its development by sensitively responding to the child's needs and signals and going along with the child's initiated activities and interactions. Using an authoritative or democratic parenting style, which is firm, yet flexible, supports children's autonomy. This will enhance family relationships, improve the atmosphere at home, and help bring out their strengths and talents, all good for making grateful kids. By taking ownership over their skills and talents and being responsible for developing them, children gain things to appreciate in life and make it easier to attract support from others, thus inviting gratitude into their daily life. Gratitude then grows naturally as children develop into their own person.

Inductive discipline supports autonomy because it teaches children how their behavior affects others and helps them understand the reasons they should treat others with respect. As they learn to make moral choices for themselves and for others, children invite positive social relationships and open the door for new sources of gratitude in their lives. This is when gratitude really becomes important, as children make more and more difficult choices that have lasting impacts on their character and course in life. With increasing independence, children turn to media. Limiting their media consumption and guiding them to use media in prosocial ways protects them from commercial influences that discourage the development of the authenticity, self-development, and social interaction necessary to grow into positive, purposeful, grateful individuals.

THEME 6: USE KIDS' STRENGTHS TO FUEL GRATITUDE

Character strengths are the virtues, or commendable qualities, that we want our children to have. Knowing and using their strengths enables a child to identify his interests and hone his skills. After you've identified your child's top strengths and you know her unique strengths profile, you should encourage and help her use those strengths whenever possible. Not only does this open up opportunities for others to contribute to the things your child loves, but it also enables him to strengthen his ability to be helpful and cooperative toward others, which will make him more grateful.

A particularly powerful way to directly promote gratitude through the use of strengths is to encourage and help your child use her strengths to thank and be kind to others. This is a great way to deepen a child's thankfulness and make her generosity more genuine and effective.

THEME 7: HELP FOCUS AND SUPPORT KIDS TO ACHIEVE INTRINSIC GOALS

It's very easy for people, especially youth, to pursue extrinsic—or materialistic goals—such as wealth, status, and image; this is a path that leads to less self-awareness because it trains youth to focus not on their own reasons for doing things, which is where appreciation begins, but on the commercial messages that bombard them. This usually leads to less fulfilling social relationships and forecloses prospects for developing deep connections with others and genuine gratitude.

As adults who care about children, it's our job to steer them away from pursuing extrinsic goals and toward pursuing intrinsic goals, such as community, affiliation, and growth. Not only will successfully achieving these goals fulfill children's fundamental human needs of competency, belongingness, and autonomy, but their growth, happiness, success, and gratitude depend on it. To amplify their gratitude even more, remember to savor their accomplishments with them along the way, and encourage them to thank those who've helped them meet their goals.

THEME 8: ENCOURAGE HELPING OTHERS AND GENEROSITY

Helping others and being generous are two key ingredients for making grateful kids. When children lend a hand, especially while using their strengths, they feel more connected to those they're helping—family and friends or people in their school and community. The practice of generosity makes kids grateful for two reasons. First, the more children give to others the more they'll learn about what it takes to be kind to others and the more they can appreciate kindness in return. Second, it helps them build healthier and more supportive social relationships, which is indispensable for developing gratitude.

Adults can encourage generosity in children by teaching them how to be more cooperative when they're playing and giving them opportunities to practice being kind. Unstructured play provides the perfect context for this vital social skill to develop. Another great way for adults to encourage generosity in kids, and thus make them grateful, is to model helping behavior for them, however small it may be. As children approach adolescence, being thoughtful with their help and empathic with friends helps them better meet friend's needs, strengthening their relationships and, thus, increasing their gratitude.

THEME 9: HELP YOUTH NURTURE THEIR RELATIONSHIPS

Strong, supportive relationships and gratitude go hand-in-hand. To make grateful children you *must* help them develop and nurture friendships and social relationships with other adults. A great way to do this is by teaching them through your actions that other people matter and that tending to relationships should be a priority.

To help children strengthen their relationships, you should encourage them to thank others regularly and to be cooperative, helpful, and giving. Savoring their relationships with others will also strengthen their bonds with people. Kids could savor the past by reminiscing, savor the present by being mindful, and, when possible, savor anticipation for upcoming events. Helping kids nurture their relationships with friends and others such as mentors, teachers, and coaches will help them build social capital. This will allow them to explore their personal strengths and the issues they care about, thus helping them develop as a person and form a sense of purpose, which is the ultimate way to deepen gratitude in life.

THEME 10: HELP KIDS FIND WHAT MATTERS TO THEM

Having a sense of purpose in life gives youth a compass for creating a meaningful life. As adults, it's our job to help kids discover their passions and to find a path to purpose that resonates with them— with their values, interests, and dreams. This starts with feeding their interests in the social issues they care about and pushing them to learn as much as they can about them. To help youth travel the path to purpose, adults can encourage them to learn how they could use their unique skills and intellectual strengths in creative and practical ways. This means finding inspiration and connecting with role models, mentors, and experts who can push them further to find and develop purpose.

The deepest sense of gratitude in life comes from connecting to a bigger picture, to an issue that matters to others and to society down the road. The ultimate gratification in life is offering up our best solutions and rejoicing, individually and collectively. In this sense, gratitude drives people to leave legacies and find fulfillment for doing so. How wonderful to put a child on a path to purpose where her reward is making her mark on the world and a never-ending stream of gratefulness.

Why Raising Generation G Matters for Society and the World

Now that we've highlighted these core themes, we'll turn to the wider picture of what all this means to us as a society. After all, trying to make grateful kids who help create the kind of world we want to live in isn't just an issue for families; it's an issue for society as well. Thus, we close with our vision for what the world could be like if together we raised *Generation G*, or *Generation Grateful*.

So how could the world be if gratitude were put into practice in the ways we described in this book? For starters, let's consider some of the immediate effects that could be expected. Imagine homes where families are in harmony. Communication is more effective because family members understand each other's goals and concerns, and conflicts aren't only prevented as a result, but resolved more quickly thanks to the anchoring their deep bond and greater understanding provide. Thanks to this anchoring, families spend more time enjoying activities together, anticipating time together, and savoring memories. They're also free to discuss the roadblocks they've encountered in pursuing their goals and dealing with their concerns. In turn, this opens up further opportunities to be supportive of each of other and invites more gratitude into everyone's life.

Imagine how schools would be different. Students come to school wanting to learn and achieve because they're confident in facing new challenges knowing they can accept success and failure. Classrooms are filled with cooperative students who are engaged because they're motivated by using their strengths, by what they've learned in school, and by wanting to make a difference to others. Teasing and hurting each other will be reduced because students are in the habit of being kind and generous toward each other, something they find rewarding. They also treat each other, as well as their teachers and other school personnel, with more respect because they feel supported in their aspirations and respected by them to begin with.

Imagine communities where kids voluntarily helped their neighbors. People unable to shovel snow would awaken to clear driveways; people going away for a long weekend would be comforted knowing that their plants were getting watered; and people who got stuck at work would be relieved knowing that their dog could be walked and fed. Coaches are reenergized to pass on their knowledge because their teams are more cohesive and driven to excel. And clergy and other community leaders have a newfound hope for the next generation because church attendance is up and volunteering has increased. Everyone wants to make a difference.

This is all what could happen sooner rather than later if we take on the challenge of raising Generation G. We *can* significantly influence the children in our own personal worlds, and, if we do, that *will* influence programs, clubs, schools, and other institutions in the community too. So we ask you to accept our challenge, and dedicate yourself to helping a child become more grateful. Our society needs this more than ever. Now's the time.

But let's see where this could lead us further in the future to really see why society desperately needs to harness the power of gratitude. Our once grateful youth have now officially become grateful adults. Many of them are married and have their own children. The relationships with their spouses and children are filled with trust, respect, support, affection, understanding, empathy, and tons of love. These same qualities also describe the friendships of this new generation. Many are also committed to service and pursuits that help make kids and communities strong and enrich our lives; these relationships with the people they help are likewise fulfilling— inspiring yet others to make a difference too.

Positive changes can also be seen in the workplaces and careers of Generation G. Business owners keep their word and support local charities; teachers use the human touch with all of their students and can count on students learning from each other more; doctors have superb bedside manners because they appreciate the importance of connecting with someone's spirit; and corporate leaders are responsible stewards of the resources they use, the communities they serve, and the future. The overall result? A society of individuals able to work together to solve the most difficult problems, a society that keeps inching toward a better world, one that can last and help us all achieve beyond our dreams.

How will *you* help shape our future?

Acknowledgments

W E ARE GRATEFULLY INDEBTED to our incredible agent, Esmond Harmsworth, of the Zachary Shuster Harmsworth Literary Agency. Esmond's ability to transform dry academic prose into something special for general audiences is nothing short of magical. We're especially grateful to Esmond for seeing promise in our proposal and agreeing to work with two first-time trade book authors. Our editor Susan Arellano, at Templeton Press, really helped shape this book by forcing us to reach deep within ourselves to better connect with our audience. We also extend immense gratitude to our other editor, Karen Kelly. With each version of every chapter we were constantly impressed by her skills to tighten our ideas and help bring the essential elements to life. Finally, we acknowledge Natalie Silver and Trish Vergilio, who helped polish the pages of our book for parents, and Matt Smiley, who helped create a book cover that had substance and that popped.

We gratefully acknowledge the generous support of the John Templeton Foundation, especially Kimon Sargeant, vice president of human sciences. Without the support of the grant from the Foundation, much of our research presented in this book, especially the four-year longitudinal study on gratitude in children and adolescents wouldn't exist. This helped us establish a foundation of research on youth gratitude. We can't possibly acknowledge the importance of the grant funding without recognizing the dedication, care, and brilliance of our mentor, Robert Emmons. Not only did he introduce us to each other, but he saw the value of our work and ideas and steadily worked with us, eventually spearheading the grant that catalyzed our research and inspired us to want to make a difference not just in academia but in society too.

—Jeffrey Froh and Giacomo Bono

· · · · ·

WITH GRATITUDE being my top character strength, I was most excited about writing the acknowledgements for this book. My deep gratitude goes to my collaborators, students, and colleagues who worked on the research described in this book. First and foremost, I'm eternally grateful to Bob Emmons. Aside from being an equal collaborator on much of the empirical research we describe, Bob has been an incredible mentor and friend over the years, showing me all of the ins and outs of academia and publishing. Thank you, Bob, for helping me fulfill what would've remained an unidentified dream. This book is because of you.

I wish to give a heartfelt thanks to my friend and coauthor, Giacomo Bono. What began as a random e-mail exchange between strangers seven years ago has turned into a very productive and exciting collaborative partnership. Writing this book was by far the most difficult professional task I've ever completed. But Giacomo's continued support made it possible, and the synergy created between us by using our unique strengths made it enjoyable. Thank you, Giacomo, for taking this journey with me. I can't wait for our next adventure!

I'm fortunate to be mentored and nurtured by several very special people. William Thieben gave me a love for learning and reading. I'm indebted to him for keeping the human touch alive and supporting me during my undergraduate years. George Giuliani gave me a rudder when I was rudderless. It's because of George that I found school psychology and my passion for wanting to help kids flourish. I'm also grateful to my friends William Sefick and Anthony Pantaleno for teaching me more about child development and school psychology than any textbook or class ever will. The research bug bit me because of Raymond DiGiuseppe and Mark Terjesen's involvement in my graduate education and their excitement for advancing the field of psychology. As Ray always said, "There's nothing like good data!"

All of our research described in this book was possible because we work with an amazing team of individuals. I'd first like to thank my many friends and fellow psychologists for being there intellectually and emotionally: Todd Kashdan, Jinyan Fan, Noel Card, Acacia Parks, Shane Lopez, Philip Watkins, Lan Chaplin, Tim Kasser, Scott Huebner, Richard Lerner, William Damon, David Shernoff, Nathaniel Lambert, Richard Gilman, Michael Furlong, and Jonathan Tudge. Alex Wood deserves special thanks for his research on the social–cognitive determinants of gratitude, which served as the theoretical foundation for our gratitude curriculum. I'm especially grateful to my Hofstra University family: Robert Motta, Paul Meller, Carol Zarzycki, Norman Miller, Sergei Tsytsarev, Lola Nouryan, Kimberly Gilbert, Amy Masnick, Charles Levinthal, Howard Kassinove, Mitchell Schare, and Charles Dill. Your encouragement and support have been unwavering since I came to Hofstra. Thank you for giving me a shot and believing in me. I also wish to thank Andrew Greene, Patrick Harrigan, and Allison Strand for helping us collect data in the schools. Without their support and dedication to helping youth thrive, much of what we know about gratitude in kids would still be a mystery. Thanks goes to my wife, Cara, and my friends, Matthew Jacofsky and Jennifer Sutherland, for reading earlier drafts of chapters and helping to make our book more appealing to parents and educators.

Countless thanks are also due to my amazing students, current and former, without whom none of this research would've been possible (in chronological order): Melissa Ubertini, Christine White, Kate Caputo, Stephanie Snyder, Pascual Chen, Lisa Wajsblat, Al-Jameela Youssef, Ashley Bartner, Jennifer Wilson, Terrance Wakely, Loren Packer, Jessica Glowacki, Vincent Conte, Danielle Ruscio, Heather Leggio, Meagan Muller, Tara Lomas, Cheray Harris, and Mikki Krakauer. Thanks also go to my first dissertation student, Katherine Henderson, for working with me to create the first version of our gratitude curriculum.

Finally, some extra-special thanks. This book exists largely because of the three most important people in my life: my wife, Cara, and my children, James and Julianne. Not only was Cara my cheerleader from this project's birth and editor in the later stages, but she was also my main source of emotional support when I didn't see any light at the end of a very long tunnel. My gratitude for her warmth and care made me work harder when I was running on fumes. Thank you, Cara, for showing me that fairy-tale romances exist. To James and Julianne, thank you for giving me so many wonderful stories to weave throughout this book; I feel privileged to have been there for each and every one. And thank you, from the bottom of my heart, for visiting me in my office while I was writing. You were never interrupting me; you were reminding me that I'm the most blessed man I know.

—Jeffrey Froh

. . . . .

MANY OF THE IDEAS in this book have been growing in my heart and mind for years thanks to the input and inspiration of so many amazing people. Some of these people shared my vision of the importance of gratitude for society and made a direct impact on my life's passion, and some were examples to live by who shaped my motivation and thinking through dedication to their calling and to me. All of these people embody gratitude as I see it; their hard work and belief in me and my dreams helped nurture many core ideas in this book. Gratitude comes from and inspires the search for more in ourselves and the trust we put in the promise of others; it is the story that opens our hearts and minds to each other and connects us to the goodness of life.

I want to start by thanking those who helped shape my motivation and thinking early on in my path. I am grateful to some professors who went above and beyond their duties to help me succeed during graduate school. Thanks go to Harvey Wichman, who introduced me to the topic of forgiveness for my dissertation research, and to William Crano, who pushed me to refine my ideas as chair of my dissertation. Their belief in me and their dedication helped me discover the value of growing positively from our relationships—a theme that resonated in my life as an immigrant and that drove me to explore further how people forge meaning in life. They helped me aim high and supported me more than they know.

Eventually, I had the pleasure of working with Michael McCullough as a postdoctoral fellow researching forgiveness and gratitude. Thanks to Mike, I discovered the transformative powers of these behaviors. It was then that I was introduced to Bob Emmons, and I'll never forget his first words to me, "Welcome to the world of gratitude." Little did I know then that gratitude held so much promise for improving people and society. My collaboration with these two brilliant scholars has been vital to me, and they inspire me to always achieve more.

Next I want to acknowledge Gregory Austin and Barbara Dietsch at WestEd. They let me apply positive youth development research to assessing youth development efforts in schools and to improving academic programs. Not only did I learn a lot about youth development and the main challenges in education, thanks to them I also was supported in my initial pursuit of a grant from the John Templeton Foundation. Around this time I also came in contact with Richard Lerner when I participated in a Summer Institute on Applied Developmental Science sponsored by the National Institute of Child Health and Human Development and the Society for Research in Child Development. Rich's visionary ideas and mentorship encouraged me to think big both for the grant and the book. He inspired me to weave together the many threads that explain why gratitude is such a potent force for optimizing youth development.

I must acknowledge my friend and coauthor, Jeffrey Froh. I, too, am always surprised by how well we work together, Jeff, and agree that the challenge of this project was surmountable because of our partnership. Quite simply, it's because of Jeff and his students and his connections with schools that I found a community in which to pursue this research and become established as a youth gratitude expert. I am infinitely grateful to him for these opportunities. Thanks, Jeff, for trusting me and letting me be a part of this wonderful journey.

Of course there are people whose influence can never be properly thanked with words. Thanks go to my friends—Mick Spitalnick, Andy and Yvonne Huffaker, and Claire Kopp—for their valuable feedback on some chapters. I am grateful to my father for teaching me generosity and persistence. Papà, you brought more goodness to the world than you were able to witness, and I know you'd be so proud. I am grateful to my mother for her unwavering faith in me and for her wisdom and strength, which bonds our family together. I appreciate my family for following Mamma's lead and having doors open and tables full; thanks to my brother Sal and sister-in-law, Jen, and to my sister Antonina and brother-in-law, John—you helped lift my spirits and reminded me to be grateful to God for giving me a second chance to enjoy life.

Finally, I save my deepest appreciation and gratitude for my wife, Kate, and my sons, Dario and Alex. Kate's input was invaluable for the book and for helping me see the many blessings in my life, especially during the most trying times. Thank you, Kate, for all the unconditional support and for teaching me to appreciate and love others. You are the greatest example I could learn from for living simply and fully at every turn. From the day we met, you lived your life and encouraged me to live mine according to the mantra, "think big," and you inspire me to do that every single day. Thank you, Dario and Alex, for the daily awe, joy, and stories you contribute to my life. I am privileged to be your dad and learn so much from you.

—Giacomo Bono

Measuring Gratitude

*H*OW TO MEASURE gratitude depends on a child's age. We divide the age ranges into three categories: three to six years old, seven to nine years old, and ten to nineteen years old. Current research in child development indicates that children can have a rudimentary understanding of gratitude as a concept at age five.

We believe, however, that given the right interaction of forces, such as applying the techniques in this book to children with certain strengths, can have a synergistic effect in developing gratitude in children. For instance, it's possible that children who have and use character strengths tied to the virtue of humanity (e.g., love, kindness, and social intelligence) or the character strengths tied to the virtue of transcendence (e.g., gratitude, hope, and spirituality) may have a particular readiness to manifest moments of genuine gratitude, even before it develops as a stable personality trait. Though we get ahead of ourselves with this untested notion, there's plenty of evidence that environments that match the needs and strengths of individuals are optimal for development.

Three- to Six-Year-Olds

No questionnaire exists for measuring gratitude in three- to six-year-olds, which makes sense developmentally considering reading and comprehension issues. Research by Nansook Park and

Christopher Peterson suggests that determining the gratitude of your three- to six-year-old can best be done by simply observing her in different social situations and with different people. As in Park and Peterson's study, children were said to be grateful if their parents described them as always saying "thank you." Beyond being polite, however, you could also look for instances of generosity and kindness toward others. Grateful youth are other-centered, always looking to lend a hand to family and friends.

Seven- to Nine-Year-Olds

The Gratitude Adjective Checklist (GAC) found on page 241 works best with seven- to-nine-year-olds. We don't have enough data with this group to tell you how your kid's gratitude level stacks up against same-age peers. We know, however, that children this age understand the questions and can answer them with minimal adult support. Further, you can compare your kid's gratitude level before you begin applying the strategies in this book by administering a pretest, and then giving the test again several months later. You can also give it repeatedly to look for any changes over time. So if you have a seven- to nine-year-old and you're interested in knowing their gratitude level or how effective the strategies are, the GAC is your best bet and follows on page 241.

Ten- to Nineteen-Year-Olds

In 2011, along with a phenomenal team of colleagues, we examined how well the existing adult gratitude questionnaires measured gratitude in kids. Working with a sample of over fourteen hundred youth ages ten to nineteen we found that the Gratitude Questionnaire-6 (GQ-6) worked best. We removed one question that was not

Gratitude Adjective Checklist

This scale consists of a number of words that describe different feelings and emotions. Read each item and then **CIRCLE** the appropriate answer next to that word.

Indicate to how much you feel this way <u>OVERALL</u>.

Feeling or emotion	Very slightly or not at all	A little	Moderately	Quite a bit	Extremely
Grateful	1	2	3	4	5
Thankful	1	2	3	4	5
Appreciative	1	2	3	4	5

Scoring Instructions: Simply sum the response for the three questions to get your child's total gratitude score. This number should be between 3 and 15. The closer your child is to 15, the more grateful they are. And the closer they are to 3, the less grateful they are.

age-appropriate, so for our purposes the GQ-6 will be referred to as the GQ-5 and follows on page 242.

Our data suggest that the GQ-5 and the GAC are great questionnaires to determine how grateful your child or adolescent is *in general.* That is, they'll tell you how grateful your kid typically is on a daily basis. Using our large data set, we'll first provide you with percentiles allowing you to gauge how grateful your child is compared to the other children who answered the questionnaire. We'll then provide an interpretation of the percentiles so you understand their importance. Keep in mind that our sample was largely Caucasian kids from very wealthy homes (when we conducted the study, the school district median household income was $94,339, and the

Gratitude Questionnaire-5

Please **CIRCLE** the number below each statement to indicate how much you agree with it.

1. I have so much in life to be thankful for.

1	2	3	4	5	6	7
Strongly Disagree	Disagree	Slightly Disagree	Neutral	Slightly Agree	Agree	Strongly Agree

2. If I had to list everything that I felt thankful for, it would be a very long list.

1	2	3	4	5	6	7
Strongly Disagree	Disagree	Slightly Disagree	Neutral	Slightly Agree	Agree	Strongly Agree

3. When I look at the world, I don't see much to be thankful for.

1	2	3	4	5	6	7
Strongly Disagree	Disagree	Slightly Disagree	Neutral	Slightly Agree	Agree	Strongly Agree

4. I am thankful to a wide variety of people (e.g., parents, teachers, other adults, friends).

1	2	3	4	5	6	7
Strongly Disagree	Disagree	Slightly Disagree	Neutral	Slightly Agree	Agree	Strongly Agree

5. As I get older I find myself more able to appreciate the people, events, and situations that have been part of my life history.

1	2	3	4	5	6	7
Strongly Disagree	Disagree	Slightly Disagree	Neutral	Slightly Agree	Agree	Strongly Agree

Scoring Instructions:

1. Add up your child's scores for items 1, 2, 4, and 5.

2. Reverse your child's score for item 3. That is, if your child scored a "7," give them a "1," if your child scored a "6," give them a "2," etc.

3. Add the reversed score for item 3 to the total from Step 1. This is your child's total GQ- 5 score. This number should be between 5 and 35.

Developed by Michael E. McCullough, PhD, Robert A. Emmons, PhD, and Jo-Ann Tsang, PhD. Used with permission.

state median household income was $43,393). Therefore, we urge you to make these comparisons knowing that the numbers should only be used as a rough guide.

Percentiles Chart for the Gratitude Questionnaire-5

AGE	25th%	50th%	75th%
10-11	28	32	34
12-13	27	30	33
14	27	31	33
15	26	30	33
16	25	29	32
17-19	26	29	32

Note: Numbers within the table represent total gratitude scores based on the GQ-5. Ages 10–11, 12–13, and 17–19 are combined because we had too few kids representing each age alone. For example, we had too few kids who were ten years old and too few kids who were eleven years old to conduct the proper analyses, so we combined ten- and eleven-year-olds.

GQ-5 SCORE INTERPRETATION

Let's use the 10–11 group as an example of how you should interpret your child's GQ-5 scores based on the percentiles chart on page 243. Go to the row for ten- to eleven-year-olds in the table, and follow along with us. A child who scores 28 out of 35 on the GQ-5 scored higher than 25 percent of the kids in our sample. If they scored below 28, then they're in the bottom 25 percent relative to the kids in our sample. A child who scores 32 out of 35 on the GQ-5 scored higher than 50 percent of the kids in our sample. If they scored below 32, then they're in the bottom 50 percent relative to the kids in our sample. And a child who scores 34 out of 35 on the GQ-5 scored higher than 75 percent of the kids in our sample. If they scored below 34, then they're in the bottom 75 percent relative to the kids in our sample. Scoring a child's GQ-5 questionnaire and reviewing the scores and corresponding percentiles in the table above will give you a good sense of how grateful the child is and perhaps how much more you need to apply the strategies in this book.

Measuring Gratitude in Adults

Several wonderful gratitude questionnaires exist for adults, the GQ-6 being one of them. Here is the GQ-6 along with scoring instructions and interpretation for your score.

Gratitude Questionnaire-6

Please **CIRCLE** the number below each statement to indicate how much you agree with it.

1. I have so much in life to be thankful for.

1	2	3	4	5	6	7
Strongly Disagree	Disagree	Slightly Disagree	Neutral	Slightly Agree	Agree	Strongly Agree

2. If I had to list everything that I felt thankful for, it would be a very long list.

1	2	3	4	5	6	7
Strongly Disagree	Disagree	Slightly Disagree	Neutral	Slightly Agree	Agree	Strongly Agree

3. When I look at the world, I don't see much to be thankful for.

1	2	3	4	5	6	7
Strongly Disagree	Disagree	Slightly Disagree	Neutral	Slightly Agree	Agree	Strongly Agree

4. I am thankful to a wide variety of people (e.g., parents, teachers, other adults, friends).

1	2	3	4	5	6	7
Strongly Disagree	Disagree	Slightly Disagree	Neutral	Slightly Agree	Agree	Strongly Agree

5. As I get older I find myself more able to appreciate the people, events, and situations that have been part of my life history.

1	2	3	4	5	6	7
Strongly Disagree	Disagree	Slightly Disagree	Neutral	Slightly Agree	Agree	Strongly Agree

Continues on next page

6. Long amounts of time can go by before I feel grateful to something or someone.

1	2	3	4	5	6	7
Strongly Disagree	Disagree	Slightly Disagree	Neutral	Slightly Agree	Agree	Strongly Agree

Scoring Instructions:

1. Add up your scores for items 1, 2, 4, and 5.
2. Reverse your scores for items 3 and 6. That is, if you scored a "7," give yourself a "1," if you scored a "6," give yourself a "2," etc.
3. Add the reversed scores for items 3 and 6 to the total from Step 1. This is your total GQ-6 score. This number should be between 6 and 42.

Developed by Michael E. McCullough, PhD, Robert A. Emmons, PhD, and Jo-Ann Tsang, PhD. Used with permission.

GQ-6 SCORE INTERPRETATION

Here are some benchmarks for understanding your score based on a sample of 1,224 adults who took the GQ-6 as part of a feature on the Spirituality and Health website.

* **25th Percentile:** Someone who scores 35 out of 42 on the GQ-6 scores higher than 25 percent of the people who took it. If you score below 35, then you're in the bottom 25 percent relative to the people who took it.

* **50th Percentile:** Someone who scores 38 out of 42 on the GQ-6 scores higher than 50 percent of the people who took it. If you score below 38, then you're in the bottom 50 percent relative to the people who took it.

* **75th Percentile:** Someone who scores 41 out of 42 on the GQ-6 scores higher than 75 percent of the people who took it. If you score below 41, then you're in the bottom 75 percent relative to the people who took

Notes

Introduction

4   *a sense of thankfulness and joy* . . . Emmons, R. A. 2004. "Gratitude." In *Character Strengths and Virtues: A Handbook and Classification*, edited by C. Peterson and M. E. P. Seligman, 553–68. New York: Oxford University Press.

4   *Gratitude can be considered* . . . McCullough, M. E., R. A. Emmons, and J. A. Tsang. 2002. "The Grateful Disposition: A Conceptual and Empirical Topography." *Journal of Personality and Social Psychology* 82 (1): 112–27.

5   *Gratitude alerts people* . . . McCullough, M. E., S. D. Kilpatrick, R. A. Emmons, and D. B. Larson. 2001. "Is Gratitude a Moral Affect?" *Psychological Bulletin* 127 (2): 249–66.

5   *Its experience and practice promotes* . . . Haidt, J. 2003. "The Moral Emotions." In *Handbook of Affective Sciences*, edited by R. Davidson, K. Scherer, and H. H. Goldsmith, 852–70. New York: Oxford University Press; McCullough et al., "Is Gratitude a Moral Affect?"

5   *Although later research hasn't* . . . Baumgartner-Tramer, F. 1938. "'Gratefulness' in Children and Young People." *Journal of General Psychology* 53: 53–66; Graham, S. 1988. "Children's Developing Understanding of the Motivational Role of Affect: An Attributional Analysis." *Cognitive Development* 3 (1): 71–88.

5   *They found that out of the twenty-four strengths* . . . Park, N., and C. Peterson. 2006. "Moral Competence and Character Strengths among Adolescents: The Development and Validation of the Values in Action Inventory of Strengths for Youth." *Journal of Adolescence* 29 (6): 891–909.

6   *Excited by this finding* . . . Emmons, R. A., and M. E. McCullough. 2003. "Counting Blessings Versus Burdens: An Empirical Investigation of Gratitude and Subjective Well-being in Daily Life." *Journal of Personality and Social Psychology* 84 (2): 377–89.

6   *the replication went on to provide* . . . Froh, J. J., W. J. Sefick, and R. A. Emmons. 2008. "Counting Blessings in Early Adolescents: An Experimental Study of Gratitude and Subjective Well-being." *Journal of School Psychology* 46 (2): 213–33.

6   *Clearly this was an area of focus* . . . Emmons and McCullough, "Counting Bless-
     ings Versus Burdens"; Lyubomirsky, S., K. M. Sheldon, and D. Schkade. 2005.
     "Pursuing Happiness: The Architecture of Sustainable Change." *Review of General
     Psychology* 9 (2): 111–31; Seligman, M. E. P., T. A. Steen, N. Park, and C. Peter-
     son. 2005. "Positive Psychology Progress: Empirical Validation of Interventions."
     American Psychologist 60: 410–21.

7   *Two recent longitudinal studies indicate* . . . Wood, A. M., J. Maltby, N. Stewart, P.
     A. Linley, and S. Joseph. 2008. "A Social–Cognitive Model of Trait and State Levels
     of Gratitude." *Emotion* 8 (2): 281–90.

7   *an actual gift-giving event among sororities* . . . Algoe, S. B., J. Haidt, and S. L.
     Gable. 2008. "Beyond Reciprocity: Gratitude and Relationships in Everyday Life."
     Emotion 8 (3): 425–29.

7   *Such assets are critical* . . . Lerner, R. M., M. H. Bornstein, and C. Smith. 2003.
     "Child Well-being: From Elements to Integrations." In *Well-Being: Positive Devel-
     opment Across the Life Course*, edited by M. H. Bornstein, L. Davidson, C. M.
     Keyes, K. Moore, and the Center for Child Well-being, 501–23. Mahwah, NJ: Law-
     rence Erlbaum Associates.

7   *They're also physically healthier* . . . Froh, J. J., C. Yurkewicz, and T. B. Kashdan.
     2009. "Gratitude and Subjective Well-being in Early Adolescence: Examining
     Gender Differences." *Journal of Adolescence* 32 (3): 633–50.

7   *We've also found that grateful teens* . . . Froh, J. J., R. A. Emmons, N. A. Card, G.
     Bono, and J. Wilson. 2011. "Gratitude and the Reduced Costs of Materialism in
     Adolescents." *Journal of Happiness Studies* 12 (2): 289–302.

10   *There are four qualities that distinguish* . . . McCullough et al., "The Grateful
     Disposition."

Chapter 1

15   *our research shows that youth* . . . Froh, J. J., C. Yurkewicz, and T. B. Kashdan.
     2009. "Gratitude and Subjective Well-being in Early Adolescence: Examining
     Gender Differences." *Journal of Adolescence* 32 (3): 633–50.

17   *Gratitude aids humans' survival* . . . McCullough, M. E., S. D. Kilpatrick, R. A.
     Emmons, and D. B. Larson. 2001. "Is Gratitude a Moral Affect?" *Psychological
     Bulletin* 127 (2): 249–66.

18   *They also reported they were learning* . . . Froh, J. J., W. J. Sefick, and R. A. Emmons.
     2008. "Counting Blessings in Early Adolescents: An Experimental Study of Grati-
     tude and Subjective Well-Being." *Journal of School Psychology* 46 (2): 213–33.

18   *Students who are satisfied with* . . . Verkuyten, M., and J. Thijs. 2002. "School Satisfaction of Elementary School Children: The Role of Performance, Peer Relations, Ethnicity, and Gender." *Social Indicators Research* 59 (2): 203–28.

24   *Knowledge of emotions* . . . Nelson, J. A., L. B. Freitas, M. O'Brien, S. D. Calkins, E. M. Leerkes, and S. Marcovitch. 2012. "Preschool Aged Children's Understanding of Gratitude: Relations with Emotion and Mental State Knowledge." *British Journal of Developmental Psychology* 31 (1): 42–56.

24   *Frustration and anger are* . . . Fredrickson, B. L. 2004. "Gratitude, Like Other Positive Emotions, Broadens and Builds." In *The Psychology of Gratitude,* edited by R. A. Emmons and M. E. McCullough, 145–66. New York: Oxford University Press.

26   *Researchers have recently discovered* . . . Fredrickson, B. L., and M. F. Losada. 2005. "Positive Affect and the Complex Dynamics of Human Flourishing." *American Psychologist* 60 (7): 678.

27   *two requirements for making sustainable gains in happiness* . . . Lyubomirsky, S. 2011. "Hedonic Adaptation to Positive and Negative Experiences." In *Oxford Handbook of Stress, Health, and Coping,* edited by S. Folkman, 200–224. New York: Oxford University Press.

29   *It's important to figure out* . . . Chida, Y., and A. Steptoe. 2009. "The Association of Anger and Hostility with Future Coronary Heart Disease: A Meta-analytic Review of Prospective Evidence." *Journal of the American College of Cardiology* 53 (11): 936–46.

29   *a "magic ratio" of 5:1* . . . Gottman, J. M. 1994. *What Predicts Divorce? The Relationship between Marital Processes and Marital Outcomes.* Hillsdale, NJ: Lawrence Erlbaum Associates.

29   *By observing seven hundred individual newlywed couples' interactions* . . . Gottman, J. M. 1999. *The Marriage Clinic: A Scientifically Based Marital Therapy.* New York: W. W. Norton & Company.

31   *In fact, he's developed a business around personal energy management* . . . Schwartz, T., J. Gomes, and C. McCarthy. 2011. *Be Excellent at Anything.* New York, NY: Free Press.

33   *If you don't regularly exercise your ability* . . . Fredrickson, B. L. 2013. "Your Phone vs. Your Heart." *New York Times,* March 23, SR14.

33   *how much time people spend feeling attuned to others* . . . Kok, B. E., K. A. Coffey, M. A. Cohn, L. I. Catalino, T. Vacharkulksemsek, S. B. Algoe, M. Brantley, and B. L. Fredrickson. 2013. "How Positive Emotions Build Physical Health: Perceived Positive Social Connections Account for the Upward Spiral Between Positive Emotions and Vagal Tone." *Psychological Science* 24 (7): 1123–32.

Chapter 2

35   *infants provide signals to parents* . . . Ainsworth, M. D. S., and J. Bowlby. 1991. "An Ethological Approach to Personality Development." *American Psychologist* 46 (4): 331–41.

36   *Attachment is the deep and enduring* . . . Ainsworth, M. D. S. 1973. "Anxious Attachment and Defensive Reactions in a Strange Situation and Their Relationship to Behavior at Home." Paper presented at the symposium Anxious Attachment and Defensive Reactions at the biennial meeting of the Society for Research in Child Development, Philadelphia; Bowlby, J. 1969. *Attachment.* New York: Basic Books.

37   *Gratitude is strongly linked* . . . Dunn, J. R., and M. E. Schweitzer. 2005. "Feeling and Believing: The Influence of Emotion on Trust." *Journal of Personality and Social Psychology* 88 (5): 736–48.

37   *When children develop a secure attachment* . . . Shaver, P. R., and C. Hazan. 1993. "Adult Romantic Attachment: Theory and Evidence." *Advances in Personal Relationships* 4: 29–70.

37   *Working models remain relatively stable* . . . Waters, E., S. Merrick, D. Treboux, J. Crowell, and L. Albersheim. 2000. "Attachment Security in Infancy and Early Adulthood: A Twenty-Year Longitudinal Study." *Child Development* 71 (3): 684–89.

38   *Minnesota Longitudinal Study of Parents and Children* . . . Sroufe, L. A., B. Egeland, E. Carlson, and W. A. Collins. 2005. "Placing Early Attachment Experiences in Developmental Context: The Minnesota Longitudinal Study." In *Attachment from Infancy to Adulthood: The Major Longitudinal Studies,* edited by K. E. Grossman, K. Grossman, and E. Waters, 48–70. New York: Guilford Publications.

38   *It's not necessarily the case* . . . Lamb, M. E. 1987. *The Father's Role: Cross-Cultural Perspectives.* Hillsdale, NJ: Lawrence Erlbaum Associates.

39   *Parents with greater empathy* . . . Dix, T. 1992. "Parenting on Behalf of the Child: Empathic Goals in the Regulation of Responsive Parenting." In *Parental Belief Systems: The Psychological Consequences for Children,* edited by I. E. Sigel, A. V. McGillicuddy-DeLisi, and J. J. Goodnow, 319–46. Hillsdale, NJ: Lawrence Erlbaum Associates.

40   *parenting styles depend on different degrees* . . . Baumrind, D. 1971. "Current Patterns of Parental Authority." *Developmental Psychology Monographs* 4(1, Pt.2), 1-103.

42   *Theory of mind is used* . . . Wellman, H. M. 2010. "Developing a Theory of Mind." In *The Wiley-Blackwell Handbook of Childhood Cognitive Development,* edited by U. Goswami, 258–84. Second edition, New York: Wiley.

43   *Research shows that language* . . . Meins, E., C. Fernyhough, R. Wainwright, M. Das Gupta, E. Fradley, and M. Tuckey. 2002. "Maternal Mind–Mindedness and Attachment Security as Predictors of Theory of Mind Understanding." *Child Development* 73 (6): 1715–26; Ruffman, T., L. Slade, and E. Crowe. 2002. "The Relation between Children's and Mothers' Mental State Language and Theory of Mind Understanding." *Child Development* 73 (3): 734–51.

47   *Character strengths are fulfilling* . . . Harrist, A. W., and R. M. Waugh. 2002. "Dyadic Synchrony: Its Structure and Function in Children's Development." *Developmental Review* 22 (4): 555–92.

52   *it helps us feel like we belong* . . . Froh, J. J., G. Bono, and R. A. Emmons. 2010. "Being Grateful Is Beyond Good Manners: Gratitude and Motivation to Contribute to Society among Early Adolescents." *Motivation & Emotion* 34 (2): 144–57.

Chapter 3

61   *how gratitude develops in adolescence* . . . This figure depicts the four basic patterns of gratitude development we found in our four-year longitudinal study of ten- to fourteen-year-olds.

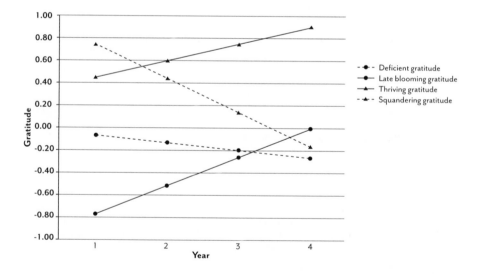

68   *These attitudes are very self-focused* . . . Emmons, R. A. 2013. *Gratitude Works! A 21-Day Program for Creating Emotional Prosperity.* San Francisco: Jossey-Bass.

69   *feel personal responsibility for their achievements* . . . Chow, R. M., and B. S. Lowery, (2010). "Thanks, but No Thanks: The Role of Personal Responsibility in

the Experience of Gratitude." *Journal of Experimental Social Psychology* 46 (3), 487–493.

70   *Supporting and encouraging kids' activities* . . . Damon, W. 2009. *The Path to Purpose: How Young People Find Their Calling in Life*. New York: Free Press.

71   *this kind of praise can hinder* . . . Mueller, C. M., and C. S. Dweck. 1998. "Intelligence Praise Can Undermine Motivation and Performance." *Journal of Personality and Social Psychology* 75 (1): 33–52.

71   *there are two basic types of people* . . . Dweck, C. S. 2006. *Mindset: The New Psychology of Success*. New York: Random House.

72   *how a fixed mindset versus a growth mindset influenced* . . . Blackwell, L. S., K. H. Trzesniewski, and C. S. Dweck. 2007. "Implicit Theories of Intelligence Predict Achievement across an Adolescent Transition: A Longitudinal Study and an Intervention." *Child Development* 78 (1): 246–63.

76   *it's worth noting that thriving involves* . . . Damon, *Path to Purpose*.

77   *the more self-control an individual exercises* . . . Muraven, M. R., and R. F. Baumeister. 2000. "Self-regulation and Depletion of Limited Resources: Does Self-control Resemble a Muscle?" *Psychological Bulletin* 126 (2): 247–59.

79   *gives us clues about where to begin* . . . Galinsky, E. 2000. *Ask the Children: The Breakthrough Study That Reveals How to Succeed at Work and Parenting*. New York: HarperCollins Publishers.

80   *Stephen Covey's* law of the harvest . . . Covey, S. 1989. *The 7 Habits of Highly Successful People: Powerful Lessons in Personal Change*. New York: Simon & Schuster.

85   *It was about a test of the human spirit* . . . Plaschke, B. 2013. "Outplaying Grief." *Los Angeles Times*, March 31, A18.

Chapter 4

89   *there were twenty-four universal human character strengths* . . . Peterson, C., and M. E. P. Seligman. 2004. *Character Strengths and Virtues: A Handbook and Classification*. New York: Oxford University Press.

89   *We're born with the capacity* . . . Seligman, M. E. P. 2002. *Authentic Happiness: Using the New Positive Psychology to Realize Your Potential for Lasting Fulfillment*. New York: Free Press.

89   *most of us become high in some strengths* . . . Shimai, S., K. Otake, N. Park, C. Peterson, and M. E. P. Seligman. 2006. "Convergence of Character Strengths in American and Japanese Young Adults." *Journal of Happiness Studies* 7 (3): 311–22.

89 *developing certain character strengths* . . . Seligman, M. E. P., T. A. Steen, N. Park, and C. Peterson. 2005. "Positive Psychology Progress: Empirical Validation of Interventions." *American Psychologist* 42 (10): 874–84.

89 *students who set personally meaningful goals* . . . Madden, W., S. Green, and A. M. Grant. 2011. "A Pilot Study Evaluating Strengths-based Coaching for Primary School Students: Enhancing Engagement and Hope." *International Coaching Psychology Review* 6 (1): 71–83.

89 *All humans share three innate needs* . . . Ryan, R. M., and E. L. Deci. 2000. "Self-determination Theory and the Facilitation of Intrinsic Motivation, Social Development, and Well-being." *American Psychologist* 59 (1): 68–78.

90 *having and valuing extrinsic goals* . . . Kasser, T. 2002. *The High Price of Materialism*. Cambridge, MA: MIT Press; Kasser, T., and R. M. Ryan. 1993. "A Dark Side of the American Dream: Correlates of Financial Success as a Central Life Aspiration." *Journal of Personality & Social Psychology* 65 (2): 410–22.

93 *These impressions then become integrated* . . . Harter, S. 1999. *The Construction of the Self: A Developmental Perspective*. New York: Guilford Press.

94 *Domains such as romantic appeal* . . . Richards, M. H., P. A. Crowe, R. Larson, and A. Swarr. 1998. "Developmental Patterns and Gender Differences in the Experience of Peer Companionships during Adolescence." *Child Development* 69 (1): 154–63.

94 *Self-efficacy, the belief in one's ability* . . . Bandura, A. 1997. *Self-efficacy: The Exercise of Control*. New York: Macmillan.

94 *Higher self-efficacy helps people* . . . Bandura, A. 2001. "Swimming Against the Mainstream: The Early Years in Chilly Waters." In *A History of the Behavioral Therapies: Founders' Personal Histories*, edited by W. T. O'Donahue, D. A. Henderson, S. C. Hayes, J. E. Fisher, and L. J. Hayes, 163–82. Reno, NV: Context Press.

96 *Having a flow experience boosts* . . . Csikszentmihalyi, M. 1990. *Flow: The Psychology of Optimal Experience*. New York: Harper & Row.

96 *flow experiences push individuals toward* . . . Froh, J. J., R. A. Emmons, N. A. Card, G. Bono, and J. Wilson. 2011. "Gratitude and the Reduced Costs of Materialism in Adolescents." *Journal of Happiness Studies* 12 (2): 289–302.

99 *The degree of discrepancy between* . . . Harter, S. 2006. "Developmental and Individual Difference Perspectives on Self-esteem." In *Handbook of Personality Development*, edited by D. K. Miroczek and T. D. Little, 311–34. Mahwah, NJ: Lawrence Erlbaum Associates.

101 *negative emotions narrow our thinking* . . . Fredrickson, B. L. 2001. "The Role of Positive Emotions in Positive Psychology: The Broaden-and-Build Theory of Positive Emotions." *American Psychologist* 56 (3): 218–26.

104   *Helping our children become resilient* . . . Masten, A. S. 2009. "Ordinary Magic: Lessons from Research on Resilience in Human Development." *Education Canada* 49 (3): 28–32.

104   *were less likely to experience depression* . . . Fredrickson, B. L., M. M. Tugade, C. E. Waugh, and G. R. Larkin. 2003. "What Good Are Positive Emotions in Crises? A Prospective Study of Resilience and Emotions Following the Terrorist Attacks on the United States on September 11th, 2001." *Journal of Personality & Social Psychology* 84 (2): 365–76.

104   *themes of gratitude for basic human needs* . . . Gordon, A. K., D. R. Musher-Eizenman, S. Holub, and J. Dalrymple. 2004. "What Are Children Thankful For? An Archival Analysis of Gratitude Before and After the Attacks of September 11th." *Journal of Applied Developmental Psychology* 25 (5): 541–53.

106   *by midadolescence friends are the major providers* . . . Furman, W. W., and D. D. Buhrmeister. 1992. "Age and Sex Differences in Perceptions of Personal Relationships." *Child Development* 63 (1): 103.

106   *One strong clue that having friends* . . . Schwartz, J. J., N. J. Kaslow, J. Seeley, and P. Lewinsohn. 2000. "Psychological, Cognitive, and Interpersonal Correlates of Attributional Change in Adolescents." *Journal of Clinical Child Psychology* 29 (2): 188–98.

106   *close friends promote the social competencies* . . . Gauze, C., W. Bukowski, J. Aquan-Assec, and L. Sippola. 1996. "Interactions between Family Environment and Friendship Associations with Self-perceived Well-being during Early Adolescence." *Child Development* 67 (5): 2201–16.

109   *even toddlers are capable of spontaneous generosity* . . . Warneken, F. 2013. "Young Children Proactively Remedy Unnoticed Accidents." *Cognition* 126 (1): 101–8.

Chapter 5

113   *Gratitude acts as a moral barometer* . . . McCullough, M. E., S. D. Kilpatrick, R. A. Emmons, and D. B. Larson. 2001. "Is Gratitude a Moral Affect?" *Psychological Bulletin* 127 (2): 249–66.

113   *While these researchers found solid evidence* . . . Bartlett, M. Y., and D. DeSteno 2006. "Gratitude and Prosocial Behavior: Helping When It Costs You." *Psychological Science* 17 (4): 319–25; Tsang, J. 2006. "Gratitude and Prosocial Behaviour: An Experimental Test of Gratitude." *Cognition and Emotion* 20 (1): 138–48; Tsang, J. 2007. "Gratitude for Small and Large Favors: A Behavioral Test." *The Journal of Positive Psychology* 2 (3): 157–67.

114   *Gratitude is our acknowledgement that a benefactor* . . . Buck, R. 2004. "The Gratitude of Exchange and the Gratitude of Caring: A Developmental Interactionist

Perspective of Moral Emotion." In *The Psychology of Gratitude*, edited by R. A. Emmons and M. E. McCullough, 100–122. New York: Oxford University Press; Heider, F. 1958. "Ought a Value." In *The Psychology of Interpersonal Relations* edited by F. Heider, 218–43. Hoboken, NJ: John Wiley & Sons; Weiner, B., D. Russell, and D. Lerman. 1979. "The Cognition–Emotion Process in Achievement-related Contexts." *Journal of Personality & Social Psychology* 37 (7): 1211–20; Zaleski, Z. 1988. "Attibutions and Emotions Related to Future Goal Attainment." *Journal of Educational Psychology* 80 (4): 563–68.

114   *people differ in how they habitually viewed* . . . Wood, A. M., J. Matby, N. Stewart, P. Linley, and S. Joseph. 2008. "A Social–Cognitive Model of Trait and State Levels of Gratitude." *Emotion* 8 (2): 281–90.

114   *Using this curriculum* . . . Froh, J. J., G. Bono, J. Fan, R. A. Emmons, K. Henderson, C. Harris, H. Leggio, and A. Wood. In press. "Nice Thinking! An Educational Intervention That Teaches Children How to Think Gratefully." *School Psychology Review* (Special Issue: Theoretical Frameworks in School Psychology Intervention Research: Interdisciplinary Perspectives and Future Directions).

117   *how young children identify common acts* . . . Bono, G., and J. J. Froh. Forthcoming. "Kindness According to Kids: A Qualitative Analysis of Children's Generosity and Appreciation." Manuscript in preparation.

121   *The above finding is consistent* . . . Hoffman, M. L. 1984. "Interaction of Affect and Cognition in Empathy." In *Emotions, Cognition, and Behavior*, edited by C. E. Izard and R. B. Kagan, 103–31. New York: Cambridge University Press.

123   *The first technique is* inductive disciplining . . . Turiel, E. 2006. "Thought, Emotions, and Social Interactional Processes in Moral Development." In *Handbook of Moral Development*, edited by M. Killen and J. G. Smetana, 7–35. Mahwah, NJ: Lawrence Erlbaum Associates Publishers.

126   *the end result of such parenting* . . . Hoffman, M. L. 1970. "Moral Development." In *Carmichael's Manual of Child Psychology*, edited by P. Mussen, vol. 2, 241–59. New York: Wiley.

126   *Love withdrawal and power assertion* . . . Brody, G. H., and D. R. Shaffer. 1982. "Contributions of Parents and Peers to Children's Moral Socialization." *Developmental Review* 2 (1): 31–75.

127   *The techniques of love withdrawal and power assertion* . . . Labile, D. J., and R. A. Thompson. 2000. "Mother-Child Discourse, Attachment Security, Shared Positive Affect, and Early Conscience Development." *Child Development* 71 (5): 1424–40.

127   *As children become adolescents they begin thinking* . . . Hoffman, M. L. 1984. "Interaction of Affect and Cognition in Empathy." In *Emotions, Cognition, and Behavior* edited by C. E. Izard, J. Kagan, and R. B. Zajone, 103–31. New York: Cambridge University Press.

128   *Another dimension of moral development* . . . Bandura, A. 2002. "Selective Moral Disengagement in the Exercise of Moral Agency." *Journal of Moral Educations* 31 (2): 101–19.

129   *a person with moral character prioritizes moral values* . . . Rest, J., D. Narvaez, M. Bebeau, and S. Thoma. 1999. *Post-Conventional Moral Thinking: A Neo-Kohlbergian Approach.* Mahwah, NJ: Lawrence Erlbaum Associates.

129   *Moral character is further strengthened* . . . Walker, L. 2002. "Moral Exemplarity." In *Bringing in a New Era in Character Education,* edited by W. Damon, 65–83. Stanford, CA: Hoover Institute Press.

129   *Self-control is* . . . Baumeister, R. F., K. D. Vohs, and D. M. Tice. 2007. "The Strength Model of Self-Control." *Current Directions in Psychological Science* 16: 396–403.

129   *individuals succeed in imposing their ultimate goals* . . . Gailliot, M. T., R. F. Baumeister, C. DeWall, J. K. Maner, E. Plant, D. M. Tice, L. E. Brewer, and B. J. Schmeichel. 2007. "Self-Control Relies on Glucose as a Limited Energy Source: Willpower Is More Than a Metaphor." *Journal of Personality & Social Psychology* 92 (2): 325–36.

130   *Children and adults interpret experiences* . . . Strasburger, V. C., B. J. Wilson, and A. B. Jordan. 2009. *Children, Adolescents, and the Media.* Second edition, Thousand Oaks, CA: Sage Publications.

131   *when young children see an ad* . . . Levin, D. E., and S. Linn. 2003. "The Commercialization of Childhood: Understanding the Problem and Finding Solutions." In *Psychology and Consumer Culture: The Struggle for a Good Life in a Materialistic World,* edited by T. Kasser and K. D. Allen, 213–32. Washington, DC: American Psychological Association.

131   *excessive television also puts children at risk* . . . American Academy of Pediatrics. 2007. "Images Kids See on the Screen [testimony]." Accessed September 2013. http://www.aap.org/en-us/advocacy-and-policy/federal-advocacy/Documents/ImagesKidsSeeontheScreen.pdf.

133   *do not put a television in their children's rooms* . . . American Academy of Pediatrics, "Images Kids See on the Screen."

133   *An American child who watches three hours* . . . Wilson, B. 2008. "Media and Children's Aggression, Fear, and Altruism." *Future of Children* 18 (1): 87–118.

133   *abundant exposure to violent programming* . . . Wilson, "Media and Children's Aggression, Fear, and Altruism."

134   *researchers found that violent video games increase* . . . Anderson, C. A., A. Shibuya, N. Ihori, E. L. Swing, B. J. Bushman, A. Sakamoto, H. R. Rothstein, M. Saleem, and C. P. Barlett. 2010. "Violent Video Game Effects on Aggression, Empathy, and

Prosocial Behavior in Eastern and Western Countries: A Meta-Analytic Review." *Psychological Bulletin* 136 (2): 151–73.

134 *exposure to prosocial content is linked to altruism* . . . Mares, M., and E. Wood-ard. 2005. "Positive Effects of Television on Children's Social Interactions: A Meta-Analysis." *Media Psychology* 7 (3): 301–22.

134 *Media consumption poses more challenges* . . . Strasburger, Wilson, and Jordan, *Children, Adolescents, and the Media.*

134 *they turn to electronic communications with peers* . . . Eagle, L. 2007. "Commercial Media Literacy: What Does It Do to Whom—And Does It Matter?" *Journal of Advertising* 36 (2): 101–10.

135 *Relationships with peers become more important* . . . Escobar-Chaves, S., S. R. Tor-tolero, C. M. Markham, B. J. Low, P. Eitel, and P. Thickstun. 2005. "Impact of the Media on Adolescent Sexual Attitudes and Behaviors." *Pediatrics* 11 (6): 303–26.

135 *media consumption has been linked to many public health threats* . . . Esco-bar-Chaves, S., and C. A. Anderson. 2008. "Media and Risky Behaviors." *Future of Children* 18 (1): 147–80; Centers for Disease Control and Prevention. 2007. *Healthy Youth! Health Topics: Six Critical Health Behaviors.* Accessed August 2013. http://www.cdc.gov/HealthyYouth/healthtopics/index.htm.

135 *Teens who showed increases in gratitude during high school* . . . Bono, G., R. A. Emmons, and J. J. Froh. 2013. "The Moral Architecture of Gratitude: If We Build It a Better World Will Come." In *Moral Formation* by W. Damon (chair). Invited talk presented at the World Congress on Positive Psychology, Los Angeles, Califor-nia, June.

Chapter 6

142 *tell the difference between a commercial and TV show* . . . Carter, O. B. J., L. J. Patterson, R. J. Donovan, M. T. Ewing, and C. M. Roberts. 2011. "Children's Understanding of the Selling versus Persuasive Intent of Junk Food Advertising: Implications for Regulation." *Social Science & Medicine* 72 (6): 962–68.

143 *effective way to ward off excessive materialism in youth* . . . Driscoll, A. M., R. N. Mayer, and R. W. Belk. 1985. "The Young Child's Recognition of Consumption Symbols and Their Social Implications." *Child Study Journal* 15 (2): 117–30.

144 *Adults who rely on "retail therapy"* . . . Arndt, J., S. Solomon, T. Kasser, and K. M. Sheldon. 2004. "The Urge to Splurge: A Terror Management Account of Material-ism and Consumer Behavior." *Journal of Consumer Psychology* 14 (3): 198–212.

144 *feeling grateful reminds us that someone cares* . . . Emmons, R. A. 2007. *THANKS! How the New Science of Gratitude Can Make You Happier.* Boston: Houghton-Mifflin.

144 *Materialistic behavior makes individuals* . . . Kasser, T. 2002. *The High Price of Materialism.* Cambridge, MA: MIT Press.

146 *materialism and gratitude are opposing values* . . . Froh, J. J., R. A. Emmons, N. A. Card, G. Bono, and J. A. Wilson. 2011. "Gratitude and the Reduced Costs of Materialism in Adolescents." *Journal of Happiness Studies* 12 (2): 289–302.

147 *You may wonder whether adopting this rule would work* . . . http://www.unicef. org.uk/Documents/Publications/UNICEFIpsosMori_childwellbeing_reportsum mary.pdf.

148 *As Peter Benson put it* . . . Benson, P. L. 2008. *Sparks: How Parents Can Ignite the Hidden Strengths of Teenagers.* San Francisco, CA: Jossey-Bass.

152 *winning the lottery or coming into a large inheritance* . . . Brickman, P., D. Coates, and R. Janoff-Bulman. 1978. "Lottery Winners and Accident Victims: Is Happiness Relative?" *Journal of Personality and Social Psychology* 36 (8): 917–27.

153 *Keeping up with the latest fashions* . . . Kasser, T., and R. M. Ryan. 1993. "A Dark Side of the American Dream: Correlates of Financial Success as a Central Life Aspiration." *Journal of Personality & Social Psychology* 65 (2): 410–22.

153 *Savoring need not be a solitary strategy* . . . Bryant, F. B., and J. Veroff. 2007. *Savoring: A New Model of Positive Experience.* Mahwah, NJ: Lawrence Erlbaum Associates.

154 *suggests a child's immersion in products tied to TV shows* . . . Linn, Susan. "Commercialism in Children's Lives." Accessed August 2013. http://www.commercial freechildhood.org/sites/default/files/linn_commercialisminchildrenslives.pdf

155 *Recall our discussion of self-determination theory* . . . Ryan, R. M., and E. L. Deci. 2000. "Self-Determination Theory and the Facilitation of Intrinsic Motivation, Social Development, and Well-Being." *American Psychologist* 59 (1): 68–78.

155 *valuing and achieving intrinsic goals* . . . Sheldon, K. M., R. M. Ryan, E. L. Deci, and T. Kasser. 2004. "The Independent Effects of Goal Contents and Motives on Well-Being: It's Both What You Do *and* Why You Do It." *Personality and Social Psychology Bulletin* 30 (4): 475–86.

156 *attaching too much importance on extrinsic goals* . . . Sheldon, K. M., & T. Kasser. 2008. "Psychological Threat and Extrinsic Goal Striving." *Motivation & Emotion* 32 (1): 37–45.

159 *materialistic people are also less generous toward others* . . . Kasser, *The High Price of Materialism.*

Chapter 7

164 *negative emotional experiences can prevent a child* . . . Raver, C. C. 2002. "Emotions Matter: Making the Case for the Role of Young Children's Emotional Development for Early School Readiness." Chicago: Harris School of Public Policy Studies, University of Chicago. Working Papers.

164 *social and behavioral competence predicts academic performance* . . . Raver, C. C., and J. Knitzer. 2002. "Ready to Enter: What Research Tells Policymakers about Strategies to Promote Social and Emotional School Readiness among Three- and Four-Year-Olds." Chicago: Harris School of Public Policy Studies, University of Chicago. Working Papers.

164 *With friendships children become their own person* . . . Asher, S. R., P. D. Renshaw, and S. Hymel. 1982. "Peer Relations and the Development of Social Skills." In *The Young Child: Reviews of Research*, edited by S. G. Moore and C. R. Cooper, vol. 3, 137–58. Washington, DC: National Association for the Education of Young Children.

167 *The more children learn to play with each other* . . . Hughes, F. P. 2009. *Children, Play, and Development*. Thousand Oaks, CA: Sage Publications.

167 *Such dramatic play in particular also supports* . . . Berk, L. E., T. D. Mann, and A. T. Ogan. 2006. "Make-believe Play: Wellspring for Development of Self-regulation." In *Play = Learning: How Play Motivates and Enhances Children's Cognitive and Social–Emotional Growth*, edited by D. Singer, R. M. Golinkoff, and K. Hirsh-Pasek, 74–100. New York: Oxford University Press.

172 *free play evolves into more mature cooperative play* . . . Parten, M. B. 1932. "Social Participation among Pre-school Children." *The Journal of Abnormal and Social Psychology* 27 (3): 243–69.

173 *Teens who kept a gratitude journal donated* . . . Chaplin, L. N., A. Rindfleisch, D. R. John, and J. J. Froh. 2013. "Reducing Materialism in Adolescents." Manuscript submitted for publication.

174 *gaining a sense of self-worth from friends* . . . Furman, W., V. A. Simon, L. Shaffer, and H. A. Bouchey. 2002. "Adolescents' Working Models and Styles for Relationships with Parents, Friends, and Romantic Partners." *Child Development* 73 (1): 241–55.

176 *mindful people are also better at communicating* . . . Brown, K. W., and R. M. Ryan. 2003. "The Benefits of Being Present: Mindfulness and Its Role in Psychological Well-being." *Journal of Personality and Social Psychology* 84 (4): 822–48.

178 *Those students who were taught how to be mindful* . . . Shapiro, S. L., K. W. Brown, C. Thoresen, and T. G. Plante. 2011. "The Moderation of Mindfulness-based Stress

Reduction Effects by Trait Mindfulness: Results from a Randomized Controlled Trial." *Journal of Clinical Psychology* 67 (3): 267–77.

179   *How we treat our partner, our children themselves, and other people* . . . Crowell, J. A., and S. S. Feldman. 1988. "Mothers' Internal Models of Relationships and Children's Behavioral and Developmental Status: A Study of Mother–Child Interaction." *Child Development* 59 (5): 1273–85.

181   *Teens are also increasingly integrating* . . . Subrahmanyam, K., and P. P. Greenfield. 2008. "Online Communication and Adolescent Relationships." *Future of Children* 18 (1): 119–46.

181   *technology's role in contemporary family life* . . . Ochs, E., A. P. Graesch, A. Mittman, T. Bradbury, and R. Repetti. 2006. "Video Ethnography and Ethnoarcheological Tracking." In *The Work and Family Handbook: Multi-disciplinary Perspectives and Approaches*, edited by M. Pitt-Catsouphes, E. E. Kossek, and S. Sweet, 387–409. Mahwah, NJ: Lawrence Erlbaum Associates.

182   *tween girls' social skills and social well-being suffered* . . . Pea, R., C. Nass, L. Meheula, M. Rance, A. Kumar, H. Bramford, M. Nass, A. Simha, B. Stillerman, S. Yang, and M. Zhou. 2012. "Media Use, Face-to-face Communication, Media Multi-tasking, and Social Well-being among 8- to 12-year-old Girls." *Developmental Psychology* 48 (2): 327–36.

183   *the challenge of removing negative uses of technology* . . . Subrahmanyam, K. and P. Greenfield. 2008. "Online Communication and Adolescent Relationships." *Future of Children* 18 (1): 119–46.

185   *can be proactive in cultivating and making use of social networks* . . . Caughy, M. O., S. M. Nettles, P. J. O'Campo, and K. F. Lohrfink. 2006. "Neighborhood Matters: Racial Socialization of African American Children." *Child Development* 77 (5): 1220–36.

185   *how social capital helps children of lower socioeconomic backgrounds* . . . Coleman, J. S. 1994. "Social Capital, Human Capital, and Investment in Youth. In *Youth Unemployment and Society*, edited by A. C. Petersen and J. T. Mortimer, 34–50. New York: Cambridge University Press; Putnam, R. D. 2000. *Bowling Alone: The Collapse and Revival of American Community*. New York: Simon & Schuster.

Chapter 8

190   *helped develop PYD theory as a comprehensive approach* . . . Lerner, R. and P. Benson. "Promoting Positive Youth Development: Theoretical and Empirical Bases." Accessed September 2013. http://ase.tufts.edu/iaryd/documents/pubPromoting Positive.pdf

XX   *gratitude and social integration mutually enhanced each other* . . . Froh, J. J., G.

Bono, and R. A. Emmons, 2010. "Being Grateful Is Beyond Good Manners: Gratitude and Motivation to Contribute to Society among Early Adolescents." *Motivation & Emotion* 34 (2): 144–57.

194 *Only 20 percent have a clear vision . . .* Damon, W. 2008. *The Path to Purpose: Helping Our Children Find Their Calling in Life.* New York: Free Press.

194 *They recognize the things they think are significant . . .* Damon, *Path to Purpose.*

194 *one of the highly purposeful adolescents said . . .* Damon, *Path to Purpose.*

195 *the parent's job is to . . .* Damon, *Path to Purpose.*

200 *are processes involved in purpose formation . . .* Damon, *Path to Purpose.*

200 *today's youth are less likely than earlier generations . . .* Flanagan, C., and P. Levine. 2010. "Civic Engagement and the Transition to Adulthood." *The Future of Children* 20 (1): 159–79.

200 *As kids become aware of political institutions . . .* Flanagan and Levine, "Civic Engagement."

200 *These actions will shape interests and pathways . . .* Flanagan, C. A., and L. R. Sherrod. 1998. "Youth Political Development: An Introduction." *Journal of Social Issues* 54 (3): 447–56.

204 *adolescence is a period of exploration . . .* Erickson, E. H. 1968. *Identity: Youth and Crisis.* New York: Norton.

204 *youth feel bewildered by the options . . .* Damon, *Path to Purpose.*

204 *more young adults are working part-time . . .* Pew Research Center. 2012. "Young, Underemployed and Optimistic Coming of Age, Slowly, in a Tough Economy." February 9. http://www.pewsocialtrends.org/2012/02/09/young-underemployed -and-optimistic/

209 *creativity and an entrepreneurial spirit are essential . . .* Pew, "Young, Underemployed, and Optimistic."

209 *research shows that creativity . . .* Harter S. 2006. "The Self." In *Handbook of Child Psychology: Social, Emotional, and Personality Development,* edited by W. Damon, R. M. Lerner, and N. Eisenberg, vol. 3, 505–70. New York: Wiley.

210 *those who consumed news media communicated . . .* Boyd, M. J., J. F. Zaff, E. Phelps, M. B. Weiner, and R. Lerner. 2011. "The Relationship between Adolescents' News Media Use and Civic Engagement: The Indirect Effect of Interpersonal Communication with Parents." *The Journal of Adolescence* 34 (6): 1167–79.

210   *commit to the steps needed to succeed* . . . Marcia, J. E. 1966. "Development and Validaton of Ego-identity Status." *Journal of Personality and Social Psychology* 3 (5): 551–58.

216   *It's therefore important for parents to realize* . . . Damon, *Path to Purpose.*

Chapter 9

220   *The ultimate function that gratitude may serve* . . . Simmel, G. 1950. *The Sociology of Georg Simmel.* Glencoe, IL: Free Press.

221   *They tend to use words like* . . . Emmons, R. A. 2007. *THANKS!: How the New Science of Gratitude Can Make You Happier.* New York: Houghton Mifflin.

Appendix

240   *children were said to be grateful if* . . . Park, N., and C. Peterson. 2006. "Moral Competence and Character Strengths among Adolescents: The Development and Validation of the Values in Action Inventory of Strengths for Youth." *Journal of Adolescence* 29 (6): 891–909.

240   *The Gratitude Adjective Checklist* . . . McCullough, M. E., R. A. Emmons, and J. Tsang. 2002. "The Grateful Disposition: A Conceptual and Empirical Topography." *Journal of Personality and Social Psychology* 82 (1): 112–27.

240   *how well the existing adult gratitude questionnaires measured* . . . Froh, J. J., J. Fan, R. A. Emmons, G. Bono, E. S. Huebner, and P. Watkins. 2011. "Measuring Gratitude in Youth: Assessing the Psychometric Properties of Adult Gratitude Scales in Children and Adolescents." *Psychological Assessment* 23: 311–24.

240   *we found that the Gratitude Questionnaire-6* . . . McCullough, Emmons, and Tsang, "The Grateful Disposition."

Index